First World War
and Army of Occupation
War Diary
France, Belgium and Germany

15 DIVISION
Headquarters, Branches and Services
General Staff
7 August 1916 - 11 August 1917

WO95/1913/2

The Naval & Military Press Ltd
www.nmarchive.com
Published in association with The National Archives

Published by

The Naval & Military Press Ltd

Unit 10 Ridgewood Industrial Park,

Uckfield, East Sussex,

TN22 5QE England

Tel: +44 (0) 1825 749494

www.naval-military-press.com

www.nmarchive.com

This diary has been reprinted in facsimile from the original. Any imperfections are inevitably reproduced and the quality may fall short of modern type and cartographic standards.

© Crown Copyright
Images reproduced by permission of The National Archives, London, England, 2015.

Contents

Document type	Place/Title	Date From	Date To
Heading	WO95/1913/2 15 Div Ops Aug 1916		
Heading	Operations. By 15th. Division against German Switch Line, August 16.	16/08/1916	16/08/1916
Miscellaneous	15th Division No. 100/4 G.a. 103rd Inf. Bde.	04/09/1916	04/09/1916
Miscellaneous	45th Infantry Brigade No. 844/G.20 Aug. 1916	20/08/1916	20/08/1916
Miscellaneous	15th Division No. 100/1g.a.	20/08/1916	20/08/1916
Miscellaneous			
Miscellaneous	Headquarters. 15th Division. Operation Report.	20/08/1916	20/08/1916
Miscellaneous	15th Division No. 100/4. G.a. 45th Infantry Brigade.	20/08/1916	20/08/1916
Miscellaneous	45th Infantry Brigade No. 837/G. 15th Division.	20/08/1916	20/08/1916
Miscellaneous	45th Infantry Brigade.	19/08/1916	19/08/1916
Miscellaneous	Patrol Report. 20/8/16. O.C. 11th A & S. Highrs. Ref. Map. encl. With Adj. 458.	20/08/1916	20/08/1916
Miscellaneous	Report On Operations On Night 12th/13th August 1916 And Subsequent Days.	12/08/1916	12/08/1916
Miscellaneous	Headquarters, 15th Division.	18/08/1916	18/08/1916
Miscellaneous	Preliminary Report On Operations Carried Out against German Switch Line 17th-18th August.	17/08/1916	17/08/1916
Operation(al) Order(s)	Addendum No. 1 to 46th Inf. Bde. Order No 87	18/08/1916	18/08/1916
Miscellaneous	C Form (Duplicate). Messages And Signals.		
Operation(al) Order(s)	Addendum No. 2 to 44th Infantry Brigade Operation Order No. 76.	17/08/1916	17/08/1916
Miscellaneous	Headquarters, 15th Division.	17/08/1916	17/08/1916
Operation(al) Order(s)	46th Infantry Brigade Order No 87	17/08/1916	17/08/1916
Operation(al) Order(s)	Addendum No.1 to 44th Inf. Bde. Operation Order No. 76	17/08/1916	17/08/1916
Miscellaneous	15th. Div. No. 100/4 G.a	17/08/1916	17/08/1916
Operation(al) Order(s)	Operation Orders. by O.C. No 4. Coy. 5th Battn. Special Brigade. R.E.	17/08/1916	17/08/1916
Operation(al) Order(s)	Addendum No. 2 to 15th. Division Operation Order No. 75.	17/08/1916	17/08/1916
Miscellaneous	A Form. Messages And Signals.		
Operation(al) Order(s)	Addendum No.1 to 15th. Division Operation Order No. 75.	17/08/1916	17/08/1916
Operation(al) Order(s)	44th Infantry Brigade Operation Order No. 76.	17/08/1916	17/08/1916
Miscellaneous	15th Division	16/08/1916	16/08/1916
Miscellaneous	A Form. Messages And Signals.	16/08/1916	16/08/1916
Miscellaneous	Headquarters, 15th Division.	15/08/1916	15/08/1916
Miscellaneous	Report On Bombing Attack By 10/11th High. L.I. on Switch Line on 14.8.16	14/08/1916	14/08/1916
Miscellaneous	Evidence Of R.E. Who Accompanied 10/11th High. L.I. In Attack On Morning Of 14th Aug.	14/08/1916	14/08/1916
Miscellaneous	9th (Service) Battalion, Gordon Highlanders, (Pioneers).	16/08/1916	16/08/1916
Miscellaneous	To, General Staff, 15th Division.	17/08/1916	17/08/1916
Miscellaneous	Headquarters, 47th Divisional Artillery.		
Operation(al) Order(s)	34th Divisional Artillery Operation Order No. 51.	16/08/1916	16/08/1916
Operation(al) Order(s)	Time Table To Accompany 34th Divisional Artillery Operation Order No. 51		
Miscellaneous	A Form. Messages And Signals.		
Miscellaneous	A Form. Messages And Signals.	17/08/1916	17/08/1916

Type	Description	Date 1	Date 2
Operation(al) Order(s)	44th Infantry Brigade Operation Order No. 75.	16/08/1916	16/08/1916
Operation(al) Order(s)	46th Infantry Brigade Order No 86.	16/08/1916	16/08/1916
Miscellaneous	Headquarters, 15th Division.	16/08/1916	16/08/1916
Miscellaneous	15th. Division	16/08/1916	16/08/1916
Miscellaneous	A Form. Messages And Signals.		
Operation(al) Order(s)	H.Q., 15th Division.	15/08/1916	15/08/1916
Map	15th Division Map No. 3. 14/8/16		
Operation(al) Order(s)	15th. Division Operation Order No. 75.	15/08/1916	15/08/1916
Miscellaneous	15th. Div. No. 100 (1)/4 G.a.	15/08/1916	15/08/1916
Miscellaneous	15th. Div. No. 100/4 G.a.	15/08/1916	15/08/1916
Operation(al) Order(s)	46th Infantry Brigade Order No 85.	13/08/1916	13/08/1916
Miscellaneous	15th Div. No. 100 (2)/4 G.a.	14/08/1916	14/08/1916
Miscellaneous	C Form (Original). Messages And Signals.		
Map	Rough Scale.		
Miscellaneous	Secret. C.C. Bde. Signals.	13/08/1916	13/08/1916
Miscellaneous	Headquarters, 15th Division.	13/08/1916	13/08/1916
Miscellaneous	15th Division No. 100 (2) /4 G.a.	13/08/1916	13/08/1916
Miscellaneous	Headquarters, 15th Division. Operation Report.	13/08/1916	13/08/1916
Miscellaneous	To The Adjutant, 12th High. L.i.	12/08/1916	12/08/1916
Miscellaneous	15th Division No. 100 (1)/4 G.a. 46th Inf. Bde. 44th Inf. Bde. 45th Inf. Bde. C.R.E. 111 Corps. 34th Division. 23rd D.A. O.C. 179th Tunlg. Coy. R.E.	13/08/1916	13/08/1916
Operation(al) Order(s)	15th. Division Operation Order No. 71.	13/08/1916	13/08/1916
Miscellaneous	44th Brigade B.M. 758	12/08/1916	12/08/1916
Map	15th Division Special Operation Map No 3 13/8/16		
Map			
Miscellaneous	Telephone Record.	12/08/1916	12/08/1916
Miscellaneous	A Form. Messages And Signals.		
Miscellaneous	15th Divn Air Reconnaissance 10.30 a.m.-11.45. a.m. 12/8/16. of the area Pozieres-Martinpuich-High Wood.	12/08/1916	12/08/1916
Miscellaneous	15th Division. No. 100/4 G.a. 46th Inf, Bde.	13/08/1916	13/08/1916
Miscellaneous	Estimated Casualties 12th H.L.D.	13/08/1916	13/08/1916
Operation(al) Order(s)	34th Divisional Artillery Operation Order No. 45.	12/08/1916	12/08/1916
Miscellaneous	15th Division No. 100/4 G.a.	12/08/1916	12/08/1916
Miscellaneous	Artillery Instructions No. 56 The G.O.C., R.A., IIIrd Corps.	12/08/1916	12/08/1916
Operation(al) Order(s)	Addendum No. 2 to III Corps Operation Order No. 108.	12/08/1916	12/08/1916
Operation(al) Order(s)	Supplementary Orders to Infantry Brigade Order No 84	12/08/1916	12/08/1916
Miscellaneous		12/08/1916	12/08/1916
Operation(al) Order(s)	46th Infantry Brigade Order No 84.	11/08/1916	11/08/1916
Map	15th Division Special Operation Map No.1. 10/8/16		
Operation(al) Order(s)	45th Infantry Brigade Operation Order No. 104	12/08/1916	12/08/1916
Miscellaneous	A Form Messages And Signals.		
Miscellaneous	Hd. Qrs. 15th Division. C.R.A. 1st Division (for Information).	11/08/1916	11/08/1916
Miscellaneous	15 Division	11/11/1916	11/11/1916
Miscellaneous	A Form Messages And Signals.		
Miscellaneous	15th Division. No. 100/3/5 G.a.	12/08/1916	12/08/1916
Operation(al) Order(s)	R.A. 23rd Division Order No. 57.	11/08/1916	11/08/1916
Miscellaneous	Lifts.		
Miscellaneous	Final Barrage.		
Miscellaneous	Bombardment.		
Operation(al) Order(s)	Amendment To 46th Infantry Brigade Order No. 84	11/08/1916	11/08/1916
Miscellaneous	S/1/83-4	11/08/1916	11/08/1916
Miscellaneous	Ninth and Last Relief. From 2 p.m. 12th August to 10.15 p.m. 12th August.	12/08/1916	12/08/1916

Type	Description	Date	Date
Operation(al) Order(s)	15th Division No. 100 (3)/4 G.a.	11/08/1916	11/08/1916
Operation(al) Order(s)	Addendum No. 1 to III Corps Operation Order No. 108	11/08/1916	11/08/1916
Miscellaneous	45th Infantry Brigade No. 717/G.	11/08/1917	11/08/1917
Miscellaneous	15th Division No. 100 (6)/4 G.a.	11/08/1916	11/08/1916
Miscellaneous	15th Division No. 100 (5)/4 G.a. 4th Australian Division. Your G.5/57 dated 11.8.16	11/08/1916	11/08/1916
Miscellaneous	Headquarters, 4th. Australian Division. 11th. August, 1916	11/08/1916	11/08/1916
Miscellaneous	15th Division No. 100 (1)/4. G.a.	11/08/1916	11/08/1916
Operation(al) Order(s)	Addendum No. 1 to III Corps Operation Order No. 108	11/08/1916	11/08/1916
Miscellaneous	15th Division.	11/08/1916	11/08/1916
Miscellaneous	15th Division No. 100 (4)/4 G.a.	11/08/1916	11/08/1916
Miscellaneous	A Form. Messages And Signals.		
Miscellaneous	15th Division No. 100 (2)/4 G.a.	11/08/1916	11/08/1916
Miscellaneous	S/1/83-2	10/08/1916	10/08/1916
Miscellaneous	Fifth Relief From 2 p.m. 11th August to 8 P.m. 11th August.	11/08/1916	11/08/1916
Miscellaneous	Sixth Relief. From 8 p.m. 11th August to 2 a.m. 12th August.	11/08/1916	11/08/1916
Miscellaneous	Seventh Relief. From 2 a.m. 12th August to 8 a.m. 12th August.	12/08/1916	12/08/1916
Miscellaneous	Eighth Relief. From 6 a.m. 12th August to 2 p.m. 12th August.	12/08/1916	12/08/1916
Miscellaneous	45th Infantry Brigade No. 710/G.	11/08/1916	11/08/1916
Operation(al) Order(s)	15th. Division Operation Order No. 73.	11/08/1916	11/08/1916
Map	15th Division Special Operation Map No. 1. 10/8/16		
Operation(al) Order(s)	III Corps Operation Order No. 108.	10/08/1916	10/08/1916
Miscellaneous	Headquarters, 14th Division.	10/08/1916	10/08/1916
Miscellaneous	15th Division No. 100/ (2)/4 G.a.	10/08/1916	10/08/1916
Operation(al) Order(s)	R.A. 23rd Division Order No. 56.	10/08/1916	10/08/1916
Miscellaneous	First Relief. From 2 p.m. 10th August to 8 p.m. 10th August.	10/08/1916	10/08/1916
Miscellaneous	Second Relief, From 8 p.m. 10th August to 2 a.m. 11th August.		
Miscellaneous	Subsequent Reliefs.	11/08/1916	11/08/1916
Operation(al) Order(s)	15th. (Scottish) Division. Preliminary Operation Order.	10/08/1916	10/08/1916
Miscellaneous	C Form (Duplicate). Messages And Signals.		
Miscellaneous	45th Inf. Bde. 46th Inf. Bde.	10/08/1916	10/08/1916
Miscellaneous	45th Inf. Bde. 46th Inf. Bde. 23rd D. Artillery.	10/08/1916	10/08/1916
Operation(al) Order(s)	Preliminary Operation Order	09/08/1916	09/08/1916
Diagram etc	Plan to accompany Preliminary Operation Order dated 9-8-16		
Miscellaneous	B.S.C	09/08/1916	09/08/1916
Miscellaneous	Headquarters, 15th Division.	09/08/1916	09/08/1916
Miscellaneous	44th. Inf. Bde. 45th. Inf. Bde. 46th. Inf. Bde. C.R.E., 9th. Gordons.	07/08/1916	07/08/1916
Map	British Trenches. German. Trenches. Sector Boundary		
Heading	Operations.-against Intermediate Line-by 15th. Div.		
Miscellaneous	45th Inf. Bde.	01/09/1916	01/09/1916
Miscellaneous	45th Inf. Bde. 46th Inf. Bde. C.R.E. Left Group D.A.	01/09/1916	01/09/1916
Map	Sketch From Air Photos		
Miscellaneous	Report Of Patrol That Reconnoitred Intermediate Line 30/8/16	30/08/1916	30/08/1916
Miscellaneous	45th. Inf. Bde. 46th. Inf. Bde. Left Group D.A. C.R.E. 9th. Gordons.	30/08/1916	30/08/1916
Miscellaneous	C Form (Duplicate). Messages And Signals.		

Miscellaneous	C Form. (Duplicate). Messages And Signals.	30/08/1916	30/08/1916
Miscellaneous	A Form. Messages And Signals.		
Miscellaneous	15th Division no. 100 (1)/8 G.a.	30/08/1916	30/08/1916
Miscellaneous	15th Division No. 100/8.G.a. III Corps.	30/08/1916	30/08/1916
Miscellaneous			
Diagram etc	Dear Henderson		
Diagram etc			
Miscellaneous	46th Infantry Brigade.	27/08/1916	27/08/1916
Miscellaneous	46th Infantry Brigade. Reference your B.M./48/16 of 27.8.16	27/08/1916	27/08/1916
Miscellaneous	Headquarters, 15th division.	27/08/1916	27/08/1916
Miscellaneous	46th Infantry Brigade.	26/08/1916	26/08/1916
Miscellaneous	45th Infantry Brigade.	26/08/1916	26/08/1916
Miscellaneous	15th. Division.	26/08/1916	26/08/1916
Miscellaneous			
Diagram etc			
Miscellaneous	Headquarters, 15th. Division. 26th. August 16	26/08/1916	26/08/1916

WO95/1913-2

15 Div Ops
Aug 1916

W. 15517—M. 141. 250,000. 1/16. L.S.& Co. Forms/W 3091/2.   Army Form W. 3091.

Cover for Documents.

No. 100/4.

Nature of Enclosures.

OPERATIONS.

By 15th. Division against GERMAN SWITCH LINE, August 16.

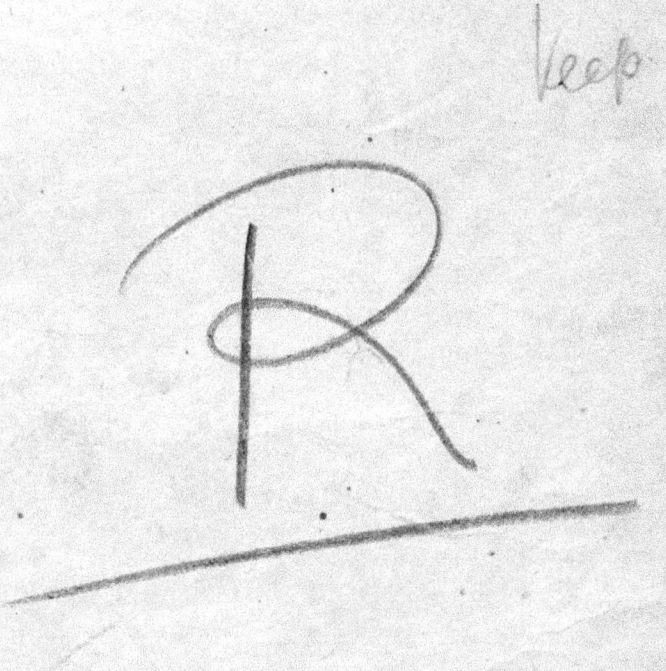

Notes, or Letters written.

SECRET.

15th Division No. 100/4 G.a.

103rd Inf. Bde.
———————————————

It is reported that requests have been made by the Infantry for the removal of the 2 inch Trench Mortar about HIGHLAND TRENCH northern end on the ground that it provokes retaliation.

If this true the G.O.C. is surprised that such a reason should have been given and he trusts you will make it clear to all concerned that it must not occur again.

So far from removing the Medium Trench Mortar support now available in that locality the G.O.C. considers that it should be increased, and the enemy works round X.6.a.2.9. kept under constant fire. He had already given instructions to this effect to Brigadier General Commanding 44th Infantry Brigade and orders were issued for putting the Brigade Headquarters in touch with the Trench Mortar Batteries to this end. He is surprised now to learn that nothing has been done. Arrangements will at once be made to bring into action at least four Medium Trench Mortars against the enemy work referred to, by direct communication between yourself and the Trench Mortar Officers concerned whom the C.R.A. Left Group D.A. will direct to report to you. Your Stokes Mortars should also maintain constant activity in this locality.

Major,

4th Sept., 1916.   General Staff, 15th Division.

Copy to :-

Left Group D.A.) For information.
44th Inf. Bde.)

45th Infantry Brigade No. 844/G.

15th Division.

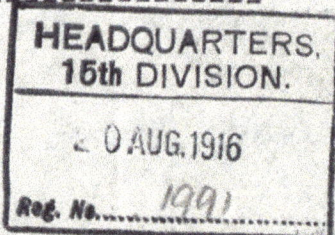

Reference your 100/1.G.a.

These strong points will be started immediately men can be found for the purpose. As the artillery barrage will have to be lengthened, I will let you know when I am in a position to start work.

The working parties will require covering parties some distance in front of them.

Brigadier - General.,
20/8/16.   Commanding 45th Infantry Brigade.

Explained to BGC on phone that there is no standing barrage.

S E C R E T.

15th Division No. 100/1 G.s.

44th Inf. Bde.
45th Inf. Bde.
46th Inf. Bde.
Left Group D.A.
C.R.E.
9th Gordons.

The G.O.C. directs attention to the following various points :-

(a). **Strong Points.** There is some misunderstanding on this subject. A distinction must be made between the few which are purely defensive and which are selected for perfecting and strengthening after the advance has passed them, and the many which are pushed forward immediately a line has been captured. The latter are to cover consolidation and to give a chain of points which can later be linked up and form a point of departure for a further advance.

The G.O.C. directs that such a chain be established without delay at least 100 yards forward of the whole SWITCH LINE from MUNSTER ALLEY to the Road in S.2.a.

The small T-heads that have been made in places along the SWITCH do **not** fulfil the above conditions. They are part of the consolidation of the SWITCH.

(b). **Liaison.** It is important that this should exist between our flank Battalion Headquarters and the flank battalions of neighbouring formations, as well as between Brigade Headquarters.

(c). **Medium Trench Mortars.** The possibility of using these in the present semi-stationary stage must have more attention. We have available the mortars of two Divisions, that is twenty four. Brigade Commanders must study the question and call for these mortars as and where necessary through their R.A. Liaison Officers.

20th August, 1916.

Lieut. Colonel,
General Staff, 15th Division.

Two hostile counter-attacks were launched against our new line.
2-45 p.m. enemy were seen to mass about M.31.d.7.5. Our Field
Artillery and Lewis Guns dispersed this movement.
Later, about 7 p.m. during the heavy bombardment of our front trenches
the enemy attempted another counter-attack which was dispersed by
our Lewis Gun fire.

SECRET.

HEADQUARTERS.
15th DIVISION.
2 0 AUG 1916
Ref. No. 1961

44th Brigade.
G.I. 257.

Headquarters,
   15th Division.

Operation Report.

Reference
   15th Divnl. Map No.3 d/14.8.16. 1/5,000.
_____

   In accordance with 44th Infantry Brigade O.O.No.75 the 7th Cameron Hrs. attacked the German trench line between the points S.1.d.4.8. and X.6.a.7.3. at 8-55 a.m. (Zero hour) on the 17th instant.

   Previous to the assault the 7th Cameron Hrs., in accordance with para. 3 (a) (1), had completed an assembly trench running from the Left Arm of GLOSTER ALLEY SAP to GORDON ALLEY joining the latter trench at X.6.a.6.1½.

   Three Assaulting Companies were in position in the assembly trench, and one reserve company in BUTTERWORTH TRENCH at 8-26 a.m.. The vacating of trenches by 9th Black Watch had also been carried out in accordance with para.3 (b) (1). The assault was made accordingly, and the trench (from X.6.a.7.3. to about S.1.d.3.8½.) was occupied by assaulting party without much opposition and with only a few casualties which occurred from M.G. fire as the enemy's trench was reached. The captured trench was cleared of the enemy very shortly. A number of the enemy were shot or bayonetted in the trench; others were shot as they retired across the open. A certain number retired across the trench past Pt. S.1.d.3.8½. When this had been done the digging parties went out to commence the construction of Strong Points in accordance with para. 3. (iv) (c). A small covering party went out in advance.

   While this was in progress a N.C.O. and 2 men of the 9th Black Watch crept out to a suspected shell hole about 40 yards North of the MUNSTER ALLEY SALIENT and captured an enemy machine gun; another enemy machine gun which attempted to come into action on the CONTALMAISON - MARTINPUICH Road was silenced by our Lewis Guns. (9-15 a.m.).

   Digging was carried on until 10-15 a.m. The parties in front were exposed to machine guns from the Cutting at S.2.a.3.5. and suffered heavy casualties accordingly.

   At this point when the officers left in the captured trench (there were three) were supervising the construction of the Strong Points, the enemy commenced bombing counter-attack along the trench. At 12-10 P.M. we held hostile trench only as far as S.1.d.2.9. where a block was constructed. This loss of trench gained was due to a shortage of bombs and the absence of officers at that point.
At 9-55 a.m. Captain Binnie, Commanding the company of the 9th Black Watch holding the Left of the SWITCH LINE, hearing that no Cameron officer remained, went up and took command of two Companies of the Cameron Hrs. He decided to construct a trench at the Eastern side of the captured SWITCH LINE. This work was begun and a platoon was withdrawn from CAMERON TRENCH to join GORDON ALLEY with the new front trench.

(1)

Meanwhile (between 9-30 a.m. and 11 a.m.) the parties constructing Strong Points were subjected to heavy M.G. and rifle fire and were forced to return to new front line. The Strong Points at S.1.b.0.3. and S.1.b.1.1. were dug down to about 2 or 3 feet. It was also found impossible to put out wire.

At about 11-45a.m. Captain MacRae and 2nd Lt. Orr, 7th Cameron Hrs., two of the officers supervising the construction of Strong Points along with Captain Binnie attempted to organise a counter-attack on the portion of the trench lost in conjunction with Stokes Mortars. The Stokes Mortar was however buried shortly after and the counter attack was not made.

About 11 a.m. Lt. Col. Marsh hearing that bombs were running short ordered two platoons of 9th Gordon Hrs. who had come up to lay trench boards to assist him. These platoons gave valuable assistance to him in conveying bombs from CONTALMAISON VILLA Dump to BUTTERWORTH TRENCH.

The consolidation of the new line was proceeded with under M.G. and rifle fire. Hostile shelling was intermittent until about 12 NOON when 8" and 5.9" shells commenced to fall on MUNSTER ALLEY and to Left of the captured line. Part of MUNSTER ALLEY was cleared. Our Lewis Guns from the new line accounted for several parties of the enemy in the ground N.W. of MARTINPUICH.

At 1 p.m. Col. Marsh came up and took over command in the front trenches.
In accordance with orders issued at 11 a.m. by the Brigade Commander Col. Marsh commenced to organise a counter attack on the portion of the SWITCH TRENCH from S.1.d.2.9. to S.1.d.5.8. Arrangements were made with 2/Lt. Anderson, 44th T. M. Battery for Stokes co-operation. One company of 8th Seaforth Hrs. which had been sent to garrison BUTTERWORTH TRENCH also came under the orders of Col. Marsh about 2-15 p.m. Arrangements were completed for the counter-attack to take place at 5-50 p.m.

Meantime, the enemy opened a barrage on the O.G. Lines about 3-30 p.m. which was maintained with a few lulls. Through the night MUNSTER ALLEY and CAMERON TRENCH were subjected to a very heavy fire.

After a successful Stokes bombardment of trenches from S.1.d.2½.9. to about S.1.d.6.8. two platoons of the 8th Seaforth Hrs. attacked the trenches from S.1.d.2.9. to S.1.d.5.8. at 5-50 p.m. from end of GLOSTER ALLEY SAP and its junction with HIGHLAND TRENCH. The trench was taken without much opposition and with few casualties. The block at S.1.d.2.9. was removed and another placed at S.1.d.5.8. Consolidation of the trench commenced at once.
About 16 of the enemy were killed and no prisoners taken.

Hostile shelling which had decreased a little about 5 p.m. at once increased; all our front trenches were heavily bombarded. This bombardment continued throughout the night.

The new line from X.6.a.7.3. to S.1.d.5.8. was now held by parties of the 9th Black Watch, 7th Cameron Hrs., and 8th Seaforth Hrs. Two companies of 9th Black Watch had become involved in the consolidation at about NOON. This line was then reorganised and a number of men were withdrawn to BUTTERWORTH TRENCH (7 p.m.). The 8th Seaforth Hrs. commenced to relieve the 9th Black Watch and 7th Cameron Hrs. in front system trenches at 9 p.m.

(2)

44th M.G. Coy. fired over 5,000 rounds during the day's operations. Many of the enemy retiring over the open were caught by our M.G. fire; in addition the attempted counter-attack from the direction of the MARTINPUICH - POZIERES Road was stopped by their fire.

44th T.M. Battery carried out successful bombardments Before the original assault, during the enemy's counter-attack, and later on the SWITCH ELBOW which latter bombardment was particularly successful in preparing it for the assault.

46th T.M. Battery assisted by bombarding the SWITCH LINE from 8-55 a.m. to 9-10 a.m.

Three Lewis Guns and one Vickers machine gun were destroyed during the operation.

One enemy machine gun was captured by the 9th Black Watch and two were destroyed by the 7th Cameron Hrs.

Bombs and S.A.A. had been arranged in suitable dumps; a further supply was carried from CONTALMAISON VILLA to BUTTERWORTH TRENCH by two platoons of 8th Seaforth Hrs.

The left Battalion of the 46th Brigade on our right was also of great assistance in bringing up bombs to GLOSTER ALLEY from their own store.

Telephone wires between companies and battalions were cut at a very early stage in the operations; communication was carried out after that by runners.

18 prisoners of the 179th Regiment were taken during these operations.

Our casualties in these operations were *up to midnight 17⁰ inst.* :-

	Officers.	O.R.
9th Black Watch.	7	170
7th Cameron Hrs.	14	243
8th Seaforth Hrs.	-	40

19th August 1916.

Brigadier General,
Commdg. 44th Infantry Brigade.

SECRET.

15th Division No. 100/4 G.a.

45th Infantry Brigade.

In view of the SWITCH East of the Railway (S.2.b.) being unoccupied by the enemy, the G.O.C. directs that you now occupy it and establish a strong post near where it crosses the road in S.2.a.

A communication trench between this part of the SWITCH and the new trench which is being pushed North East from 70th AVENUE, to be made without delay.

2. Above in confirmation of telephone conversation with your Brigade Major and with reference to your 837/G dated 20.8.16.

20th August, 1916.

Lieut. Colonel,
General Staff, 15th Division.

Copy to :-
Left Group R.A. (for information).

SECRET.   45th Infantry Brigade No. 837/G.

15th Division.

> HEADQUARTERS,
> 15th DIVISION.
> 20 AUG. 1916
> Reg. No. 1982

Herewith report from patrol sent out last night. This patrol was intended to have gone out at 5.30 p.m. It appears that at any time I can occupy the GERMAN SWITCH LINE up to the road at S.2.a.7.1., but if the Division on our right does not conform, my right flank would be rather in the air, and also in a hollow.

                         Brigadier - General.,
20th August 1916.   Commanding 45th Infantry Brigade.

L.A. 130.

Headquarters,
　45th Infantry Brigade.

　　　　　Attached patrol report on special reconnaissance speaks for itself. A message was sent the O. C. Coy. at 11.30 p.m. that the artillery barrage which had been stopped since 5.30 p.m. must come on again, and that he had better get his patrol in or cancel it if it was unable to get out. You were advised to that effect shortly after. If the barrage was continued again it would appear as if it had not affected patrol.

　　　　　　　　　　　　　sd/ A. J. CAMPBELL, Lt. & Adjt.
　　　　　　　　　　　　　　　　for Lieut - Colonel.,
19th August 16'.　　Commanding 11th Bn. A & S. Highlanders.

Patrol Report.　　　　　　　　　　　　20/8/16.

TO:-
O. C. 11th A. & S. Highrs.

Ref. Map. encl. with Adj. 458.

As ordered, an officers patrol was sent out to examine and report on the GERMAN SWITCH LINE from its junction with RAILWAY Pt. S.2.c.½.9. to the East.

The patrol consisting of one Officer, one L/C. and one private left continuation of WELCH ALLEY (about Pt. S.1.d.9.8.) at 11.45 p.m. 19th and worked along our side of SWITCH LINE, at a maximum distance of 15 yards from the parapet as far as - approximately - Pt. S.2.b.0.4. On their way the patrol entered the SWITCH 6 times, moving on each occasion with freedom up and down the trench. No signs of recent occupation, and the patrol was not molested in any way. The trench between S.1.d.9.8. and about S.2.a.7.1. is pretty deep and affords good cover. Eastwards from this however it is badly battered, amd mostly flat.

The patrol reports that the enemy's lights were being put up from Pts. about 100 yards to 150 yards in rear of the SWITCH, where it is presumed their line lies.

The patrol crossed the SWITCH LINE but was <u>unable</u> to push on as far as SUNKEN ROAD, about S.2.a. central.

Patrol returned safely at 1.35 a.m. (20th) about Pt. S.2.c.5.5.

　　　　　　　　　　sd/ A. SHEWAN.　　　　　　　Captain.,
　　　　　　　　　　　O. C. "A". Company.

X Presumably our Barrage was the reason.

REPORT ON OPERATIONS

ON

NIGHT 12th/13th AUGUST 1916

AND SUBSEQUENT DAYS.

-

1. The relief of the 13th ROYAL SCOTS by the 6TH CAMERON HIGHLANDERS was completed by 9.45 a.m. on the 12th inst.

2. At 6 p.m., the 6/7th ROYAL SCOTS FUSILIERS moved up and occupied the trenches left vacant by the 6th CAMERON HIGHLANDERS as this battalion closed to its left into a position of assembly.

3. About 10.15 p.m., the first and second waves began to move out into position in " NO MAN'S LAND ". A tape had been stretched parallel to the front to be assaulted, and about 150 yards from it. This proved of great assistance. The first wave when formed on the tape crawled forward 10 yards leaving room for the second wave to form on the tape. As far as can be ascertained no casualties were suffered during these preliminary movements, our artillery maintaining the usual nights barrage on the GERMAN SWITCH LINE, and in rear of it.

4. At 10.30 p.m. (ZERO), the artillery opened an intense bombardment, the objective being as during the normal barrage. At the same time the Infantry started to move forward, and at 10.32 p.m. reached their objective. The artillery bombardment was most effective, and all ranks advanced with confidence right under the barrage.

5. At 11.50 p.m. A wire was received that the SWITCH was occupied by 3 companies 6/7th ROYAL SCOTS FUSILIERS. This afterwards proved to be incorrect.

At 11.54 p.m. The O. C. 6th CAMERON HIGHLANDERS reported that there had been great difficulty in finding the SIWTCH, but that his companies had reached what appeared to be the SWITCH line and were digging in.

At 12.23 a.m. Report received from the 46th INFANTRY BRIGADE that the H. L. I. had not got into the SWITCH.

At 12.28 a.m. The O. C. 6/7th ROYAL SCOTS FUSILIERS was ordered to bomb to his right and that the order forbidding this no longer held good, as the 46th INFANTRY BRIGADE had not got into the SWITCH. A block to be made and offensive bombing along the SWITCH to the East.

At 12.58 a.m. All companies of the 6th CAMERON HIGHLANDERS reported in touch and digging in.

At 1.40 a.m. Owing to a message that the 46th INFANTRY BRIGADE would attack again, and also that the 6/7th ROYAL SCOTS FUSILIERS were suffering from machine gun fire from our right, orders were sent that 6/7th ROYAL SCOTS FUSILIERS were to hold on at all costs.

At 2 a.m. The O. C. 6/7th ROYAL SCOTS FUSILIERS, having reinforced his right with a company, orders were issued for O. C. 11th A & S. HIGHLANDERS to move one company from GOURLAY TRENCH to BUTTERWORTH TRENCH, and one company from CONTALMAISON to GOURLAY TRENCH.

At 2.20 a.m. O. C. 6/7th ROYAL SCOTS FUSILIERS reported his left company in touch with the 6th CAMERON HIGHLANDERS, and that it and his centre company were digging in, but the situation on his right was not clear.

At 2.30 a.m. Message received that 46th INFANTRY BRIGADE would not attack again.

At 2.35 a.m. O. C. 6th CAMERON HIGHLANDERS reported his line continuous.

At 2.40 a.m. Orders were sent to 6/7th ROYAL SCOTS FUSILIERS and 6th CAMERON HIGHLANDERS to thin out their line before dawn, and hold it with Lewis and Vickers guns.

(2).

7. On August ~~14th~~ 13th the line was further consolidated. Very considerable casualties were inflicted on the enemy owing to the extensive view which could be obtained from the position gained - especially on the night of August 14th/15th when the enemy was observed advancing from the direction of the RAILWAY running from MARTINPUICH towards the WINDMILL with a view either of relieving or ~~concentrating~~. Counterattacking.

N O T E S.

1. The artillery barrage was excellent. The infantry advanced close up to it, and suffered no loss from our shell fire.
 The Australian Division on our left gave considerable help and assisted the 6th CAMERON HIGHLANDERS in the consolidation of MUNSTER ALLEY. The 9th GORDON HIGHLANDERS worked very hard and completed the communication trench by daylight August 13th.

2. The Infantry advance lost direction and bore too much to our left in spite of the fact that the probability of this had been realized and the tape pushed forward on the left.

3. Considerable difficulty was experienced in stopping the men and making them realize exactly what they had to do. In spite of most careful previous instructions, one company of 6th CAMERON HIGHLANDERS went much too far.

4. The non success of the Brigade on our ~~left~~ right to a great extent prevented the whole of our objective being gained, and was probably the cause of our right coming under heavy machine gun fire.

5. The formation adopted appeared suitable, but a deeper formation would of course been adopted had the objective been more than one line of trench.

6. Orders were issued for strong points to be constructed in front of the position gained, but owing to the fall of the ground in front of the SWITCH sloped away, these strong points were not considered necessary by Officers on the spot, and afterwards were ordered to be made in rear of the line. I agreed to this.

7. Although the new position gained gave an excellent view and splendid artillery observation, no artillery officer was seen in the front line till 4 p.m. August 13th., and then with no means of communication. This seems wrong in view of a possible counter-attack, or even in the ordinary course of artillery duties.

8. All officers must take bearings or other steps to ensure direction, and it was found that if men are not almost shoulder to shoulder that they loose direction very quickly in the dark.

9. Rear waves should carry consolidating material and tools. The front wave should not, but should go as light as possible.

10. Nearly all the casualties were suffered by M. G. Fire from our right front, or by rifle fire after the objective was gained.

12. It is suggested that machine and Lewis gunners should carry bombs as it was found that the enemy crept forward from shell hole to shell hole, and were able to get within bombing distance of the advanced guns. The result was that the machine gunners had to borrow bombs from others, which were used with excellent effect in bolting the enemy from his cover and causing him to give an excellent target for the guns.

(3).

12. Burial parties must be sent forward as soon as the situation permits.
    This duty must not be done by those who should work on the consolidation of the captured trenches. In this case this was ommitted and caused delay.

[signature]

Brigadier - General.,
Commanding 45th Infantry Brigade.

17/8/16.

Headquarters,
    15th Division.

    The attached report by O.C. 10/11th High.L.I. (Left Battalion) on operations against SWITCH LINE is forwarded.

                                Brig. General.

Brigade H.Q.   Commanding.
    18th Aug. 1916.   46th Inf.Bde.

Preliminary Report on Operations carried out against
German SWITCH LINE 17th - 18th August.

About 6 p.m. last night the Seaforths attacked the German SWITCH LINE W. of the SWITCH ELBOW and bombed their way eastwards along it. One company of the 10/11th High.L.I. taking advantage of the opportunity joined them in small parties from H.L.I. trench and the enemy was driven along towards the railway and a block was established about 120 yards E. of the SWITCH ELBOW. The enemy meanwhile created a barrage right down and across our communications behind, which continued for an hour. The 10/11th High.L.I. dug H.L.I. Trench through to the SWITCH and carried up S.A.A. bombs, R.E. material, Very lights, etc. About 8.15 p.m., O.C., 10/11th High.L.I. from information received, arranged for the barrage to lift 75 yards for 150 yds. E. of the ELBOW. Report later from the front line show that this was the opportune moment, for the enemy, by this time disorganised, had taken to the open only to find themselves in the midst of the lifted barrage. The work of consolidation commenced. The SWITCH LINE proved to be wide and rather shallow. Also it had been, in parts, almost obliterated by our bombardments. Sandbags were filled and every effort was made to construct a serviceable trench out of the wreck. A strong bombing block was established on the right and four Lewis Guns taken forward to help hold the line, the Vickers remaining for defensive purposes in our old fire-trench. The work of carrying and digging was much interrupted and impeded by shell fire, but good progress was made and by daylight H.L.I. trench had been made into a useful communication and the (left pusher sap) was dug through although very shallow in most places. During the night the Seaforths sent out patrol covering the whole front of the SWITCH LINE. Patrol came upon isolated parties of Germans taking refuge in shell holes, but these fled at their approach. They reported the whole area incredibly broken up by shell fire.

During the night also a company of 10th Sco. Rif. occupied KOYLI TRENCH vacated by our company when it moved up. Early this morning reconnoitring of the SWITCH LINE beyond our block commenced and 10 of the enemy gave themselves up. It was arranged that a party of one officer and 25 men from the 10th Sco.Rif. should, if no opposition were encountered, create a strong point about 50 yards west of the Railway. A party consisting of one N.C.O. and 2 men preceeded them and again reconnoitred the trench where three more prisoners were taken. All these belonged to the 179th (Saxon (Regt. of Infantry.

LEAN SAP

18th August, 1916.

(Sgd) R.F. FORBES, Lt.Col.
Commanding, 10/11th High.L.I.

SECRET   Copy No ...

ADDENDUM NO. 1 to 46th Inf.Bde. Order No 87

**HEADQUARTERS
15th DIVISION.
18 AUG 1916
Reg. No. 1943**

1. Zero hour will be at 2.45 p.m.

2. There is to be no action which might cause the enemy to be specially alert between the conclusion of the special bombardment at 10 a.m. and zero. Normal activity will continue.

3. At zero hour the Left Group Divisional Artillery will conform with the bombardment being carried out with the Division on our right by bombarding portions of the SWITCH LINE still in enemy hands. Timings :—

    Zero — 30 yds in front of the objective.
    0.30 seconds — Lift onto SWITCH LINE and remain there.

4. (a) The smoke discharge will begin at Zero along the whole front and will last for 20 minutes.

  (b) During the discharge the line is to be thinly held.

  (c) Lewis and Machine Guns to be active.

  (d) If smoke is not to be discharged Battalions will be informed by the code words " Tobacco not to be issued "

5. (a) All units will stand to arms from 2.30 p.m. keeping under cover where possible.

  (b) O.C., 7/8th K.O.Sco.Bord. will be careful to work in close co-operation with left battalion of 1st Infantry Brigade.

6. Zero time for this operation is not to be telephoned or wired.

                                         Captain,
                                         Bde Maj.
                                       46th Inf.Bde.

Issued at 6 30 a
   through Signals.

Copy No	
1	File
2	War Diary
3	7/8th K.O.Sco.Bord.
4	10th Sco.Rif.
5	10/11th High.L.I.
6	12th High.L.I.
7	46th M.G.Coy
8	46th T.M.Bty
9	73rd Coy. R.E.
10	"G" Coy. 9th Gordons
11	Medium T.M.Bty
12	178th(T) Coy, R.E.
13	44th Inf.Bde.
14	1st Infantry Brigade
15	15th Division.

"C" Form (Duplicate).
MESSAGES AND SIGNALS.

Army Form C. 2123.
(In books of 50's in duplicate.)

No. of Message ....

| | Charges to Pay. | Office Stamp. |
| | £ s. d. | |

Service Instructions.

Handed in at .... Office .... m. Received .... m.

TO O.C.

| Sender's Number | Day of Month | In reply to Number | AAA |
| M.752 | 18 | | |

Reference O.C. no 87 AAA pass to your right will hold LANCS SAP and LANCS TRENCH from LANCS SAP to road keeping through S.E.C. till further orders AAA Divn on my right has now taken over responsibility for Special RE work in LANCS SAP AAA Inform RE Officer in charge AAA added to distrbn O.U. and O.B.

8.53 a.m.

FROM M V
PLACE & TIME 5.30 a.m.

Wt. 432—M437. 500,000 Pads. H W V 5/16 Forms C.2123.

**HEADQUARTERS,
15th DIVISION.
18 AUG. 1916**
Reg. No.

S E C R E T.   Copy No. 10

Addendum No.2 to 44th Infantry Brigade Operation Order No.76.
_____

17-8-16.

1.   Reference para 5.
        Time for bombardment on August 18th.
        8 A.M. to 10 A.M.
     instead of as therein stated.

2.   Reference para 6.
        Five minutes intense bombardment will be 9-30 A.M.
        not 1-30 P.M.

3.   No attempt is to be made by the Infantry to induce the
     enemy to expect an attack at 9-30 A.M.

Issued to   Major,
   Recipients of O.O.76.   Brigade Major,
   Through Signals.   44th Infantry Brigade.
   9-45 P.M.

Headquarters,
    15th Division.

On close investigation of photograph 34.c.153 dated 16th inst. and after inspection of the ground I find that 70th AVENUE has only been dug to a point about 2½ inches from the West edge of road (measured at right angles to road).

The remainder which appears like trench on photograph is really only tracing tape, and I am altering the direction from 2 p.m. to-day from that point.

I fear that unless the enemy keep their guns quiet to-night it will be quite impossible to complete the trench by to-morrow morning as the last two nights it has been impossible to work out there for any length of time owing to hostile Artillery fire.

Brigade H.Q.
17 August, 1916.

Brig.Gen.
Commanding,
46th I.Bde

4.45p. It has been impossible to carry on work since 2p owing to enemy art. fire

SECRET   Copy No. 15

**HEADQUARTERS,
15th DIVISION.
17 AUG 1916
Reg. No. 1926**

46th Infantry Brigade Order No 87

17-8-16.

1. On the 18th inst: the Right Division is attacking, among other objectives the INTERMEDIATE LINE, from the road in S.2.d. to S.2.d.7.4.

2. (a) The 15th Division will co-operate on the 18th inst. by the discharge of smoke for 20 minutes on the front S.2.c.3.7.

   (b) The instructions regarding the discharge of this smoke have been issued to 10/11th High.L.I. and 7/8th K.O.Sco.Bord., a copy is attached for 12th High.L.I.

   (c) The actual hour at which the smoke discharge will commence will be communicated later.

   (d) One section 4 Coy, 5th Bn Special Brigade R.E. will assist with 4 inch Stokes Mortars.

3. (a) A deliberate bombardment of the objective began at 5 p.m. on August, 16th and continues to Zero on the 18th.

   (b) There are also special bombardments on 16th, 17th and 18th instants as described in B.M./6/4 dated 16th inst.

4. A "Chinese" attack will be carried out at 1.30 p.m. on 18th as described in B.M./6/4 para 7. *Cancel*

5. At an hour to be notified later the Barrett Jack in LANOS SAP will be exploded. O.C. Right Sub-section will at once complete LANOS SAP through to the INTERMEDIATE LINE and will have a digging party and a covering party all ready organised for this purpose.

6. O.C. Medium Trench Mortar Battery, and O.C. 46th Trench Mortar Battery and O.C. 46th Machine Gun Company will be prepared to co-operate on that portion of the INTERMEDIATE LINE running North along the E. side of the road in S.2.c. and that portion of the SWITCH LINE to the North of the INTERMEDIATE LINE.

7. Each unit will send a representative to Brigade Headquarters at ~~7 a.m.~~ *12 noon* on the 18th inst. for watches to be synchronised. *11 am*

8. Zero hour will be communicated later.

Captain,
Bde Maj.
46th Inf.Bde.

Issued at 5/p
through Signals.

Distribution overleaf.

SECRET   Copy No ..

                        46th Infantry Brigade Order No 87

                                                                        P=B=D.

1. On the .... of the Right Division is attacking,
among other objectives the INTERMEDIATE LINE, from the
road in S.2.d. to S.2.d.7.5.

2. (a) The 15th Division will co-operate on the 19th
inst. by the discharge of Smoke and Gas 10 minutes on the
front S.21.d.7.

   (b) The Inf .... the .... are discharge of
this smoke have been .... as follows: 7/8th K.O.S.B. and
7/8th K.O.Sco.Bord. .... for 10th High.L.I.

   (c) ....e smoke discharge
All commence all ....

   (d) Gas section .... Special Brigade
R.E. will assist 46th s ....

3. (a) A deliberate bombardment of the objective
begun at 5 p.m. on August 18th and continues to zero
on the 19th.

   (b) There are also special bombardments on
18th, 19th and 20th instants as described in Bn's/G/4
dated 17th inst.

4. A "Chinese" attack will be carried out at
1.30 p.m. on 19th as described in B/G/8 para 7.

5. As an hour to be notified later the Sappers from
1.WOS SAP will be employed, O.C. Right Sub-section
will at once complete L.WOS SAP through to the
INTERMEDIATE LINE and will have a digging party and a
covering party all ready organised for this purpose.

6. O.C. Medium Trench Mortar Battery, MMS O.C.
46th Trench Mortar Battery and O.C. 46th Machine Gun
Company will be prepared to co-operate on that portion
of the INTERMEDIATE LINE running North along the E.
side of the road in S.2.c. and that portion of the
S DITCH LINE to the North of the INTERMEDIATE LINE.

7. Each will send a representative to
Brigade Headquarters at 7 a.m. on the 19th inst. for
watches to be synchronised.

8. Zero hour will be communicated later.

                                          Captain,
                                          Bde Maj.
Issued at   46th Inf.Bde.
through Signals.

Distribution overleaf.

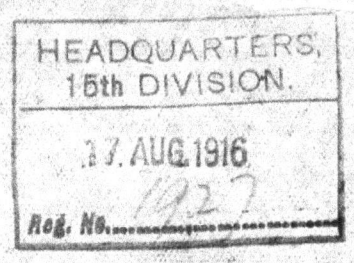

HEADQUARTERS,
15th DIVISION.
17. AUG 1916
Reg. No. 1927

S E C R E T.

44th Brigade.
B.M. 835

Addendum No.1 to 44th Inf. Bde. Operation Order No.76.

1. The Zero hour will be 2-45 p.m. at which hour the Smoke discharge will commence.

2. Watches will be synchronised at 11 a.m. on the 18th and not 8 a.m. as previously stated.

3. During the discharge of Smoke the line is to be thinly held. Lewis and Machine Guns to be active.

4. Zero time for this operation is not to be telephoned or wired.

17th August 1916.

Major,
Brigade Major,
44th Infantry Brigade.

To/
All recipients of 44th I.B. Operation Order No.76 d/17.8.16.

SECRET.

15th. Div.
No.1007/4 G.a.

44th. Inf. Bde.   15th. Div. Arty.
45th. Inf. Bde.   34th. Div. Arty.
46th. Inf. Bde.   47th. Div. Arty.
9th. Gordons.   C.R.E.
A.D.M.S.

Owing to further advance in SWITCH LINE, in paragraph 4 of Addendum No. 2 to 15th. Division Operation Order No.75 for "S.1.d.5.8" read "S.1.d.7.8".

HEADQUARTERS,
15th DIVISION.
17 AUG. 1916
Reg. No.

[signature]

Lieut. Colonel.
General Staff, 15th. Division

Copy to :-
    III Corps.
    III Corps Artillery.
    III Corps Heavy Arty.

Copy No 2.

Operation Orders
by O.C. No 4. Coy 5th Battn
Special Brigade. R.E.

HEADQUARTERS, 15th DIVISION.
AUG. 1916
Reg. No. 1919

1. Sections "N" & "P" of No 4. Coy under the command of Lieuts WISDOM, & Mac NAMEE respectively will make a smoke barrage with 4" Stoke's Mortars on the 18th inst lasting from Zero to Zero + 20.

2. (a). Section "N" Sub-Sections 38. & 39.
   Sub-Section 39. with 4. guns. will fire from emplacements in & about S.2.c.2.4 These guns will barrage to hide observation from & behind enemy trench S.2c.0.9 to S.2a.7.1.
   Sub-Section 38 with 4 guns, will fire from emplacements in & about S.1.D.3.4. & will barrage to hide observation from & behind enemy trench S!d.3.8 to S.2c.0.9

   (b). Section "P" Sub-Sections 43 & 45.
   Sub-Section 43. with 3. guns will fire from emplacements in & about X.6.a.7.3.
   Sub-Section 45. with 3. guns will fire from emplacements in & about X6a. 5.6
   These 6. guns will barrage from R.36.c.7.2 to S!b.3.1. — Sub Section 43. covering the right sector; Sub-Section 45. the left sector.

3. Number of rounds per gun :- 20.

4. Two orderlies from each of Sub-Sections 43. & 45. will report to O.C. No 4. Coy at left Bde H.Q. at 12.45 p.m. on 18th inst

P.T.O

continued

Two orderlies from each of sub-sections 38 & 39. will report to Lieut. Bradley V.C. at right Bde. H.Q. at 12.45. p.m. on 18th inst.

5. At 12.45 p.m. O.C. No. 4. Coy. & Lieut. Bradley will decide whether the wind is favourable or not.

6. This information will be immediately communicated to O's. C. Sections, & Sub-Sections at 12.45 p.m. by Orderlies. See para 4.

7. Watches will be synchronised by an N.C.O from each sub-section at respective Bde. H.Q's at 1 pm.

8. O's. C. sections will use their own discretion as to time of withdrawal of guns, & personnel, after barrage has been completed.

9. O's. C. Sections must be in touch with O's. C. battalions in their respective fronts.

Copy No 1. 3rd Corps.
    2. 15th Division
    3. 44th Bde.
    4. 46th Bde
    5. O.C. 5th Bn Sp. Bde. R.E.
    6. Lieut. Bradley. V.C.
    7. Lieut. Wisdom
    8. Lieut. MacNamee
    9. File.

A. E. Kent Capt.
O.C. No 4 Coy.
5th Battn Sp. Bde. R.E.

17/8/16

Copy No. _____

--- Addendum No.2 to 15th. Division Operation Order No.75. ---

Headquarters,
15th. Division.
17th. August 1916.

Reference paragraph 3 of 15th. Division Operation Order No.75.

1. The special bombardment of the INTERMEDIATE and SWITCH LINES on the 18th. will take place from 8.a.m. to 10 a.m., instead of 10 a.m. to 2 p.m.

2. Zero for the 5 minutes intense bombardment will be 9.30 a.m. not 1.30 p.m.
There will be 5 minutes intense fire from minus 5 minutes to Zero. At Zero the fire will lift; it will jump back suddenly at Zero + 90 seconds.

3. No attempt is to be made by the Infantry to induce the enemy to expect an attack at 9.30 a.m. Everything is to be normal until 2.45 p.m. (vide Addendum No.1.)

4. No heavy Artillery will fire on the German SWITCH LINE during the special bombardment but 18 prs and 4.5" howitzers will bombard that line east of S.1.d.5.8. All trenches and saps within 200 yards of the INTERMEDIATE LINE will be vacated between 8 a.m. and 10 a.m.
The front to be covered by machine gun and Lewis gun fire.

5. Signal time will not now be distributed at 7 a.m. as was ordered in paragraph 4 of Operation Order No.75.

H. Knox
Lieut. Colonel.
General Staff, 15th. Division.

S.1.d.7.8
corrected by 100/4 Inf
d/17/8/16

Issued at 4.40 p.m.
to :-

III Corps. ...	Copies Nos.1 & 2.	15th. Div. Arty. ...	Copy No.12.
III Corps Arty..	Copy No. 3.	34th. Div. Arty. ...	,, 13.
III Corps H.A...	,, 4.	47th. Div. Arty. ...	,, 14.
1st. Division...	,, 5.	C.R.E. ...	,, 15.
1st. Aust.Div...	,, 6.	A.D.M.S. ...	,, 16.
44th. Inf. Bde..	,, 7.	A.P.M. ...	,, 17.
45th. Inf. Bde..	,, 8.	"A" & "Q". ...	,, 18.
46th. Inf. Bde..	,, 9.	War Diary. ...	,, 19.
9th. Gordons. ..	,, 10.	File. ...	,, 20.
15th. Signals...	,, 11.	4th.Co.5th.Bn.Spec Bde. R.E....	,, 21.

"A" Form.
Army Form C. 2121.
MESSAGES AND SIGNALS. No. of Message_____

| Prefix_____Code_____m. | Words | Charge | This message is on a/c of: | Recd. at_____m. |
| Office of Origin and Service Instructions. | Sent At_____m. To_____ By_____ | | _____Service. (Signature of "Franking Officer.") | Date_____ From_____ By_____ |

TO { All recipients of Addendum No. 1.

Sender's Number.	Day of Month	In reply to Number	A A A
G.127.	17th.		

Ref. Addendum No. 1 to 15th Div. O.O.75 subpara (b) for "minutes" read "seconds" AAA Addressed all concerned.

From 15th Div.
Place
Time 6.10 p.m.

The above may be forwarded as now corrected.
(Z)
Sd. H. KNOX, Lt. Col. G.S.
Censor. Signature of Addressor or person authorised to telegraph in his name.
* This line should be erased if not required.

Copy No._____

Addendum No.1 to 15th. Division Operation Order No.75.

Headquarters,
15th. Division.
17th. August 1816.

Reference paragraph 2 of 15th. Division Operation Order No.75 :-

The 15th. Division will co-operate as below in the operations which are being undertaken on the 18th. instant by the Division on our right.
Zero hour will be 2.45 p.m.

(a). There is to be no action which might cause the enemy to be specially alert between the conclusion of the "Chinese" attack and Zero. Normal activity will continue.

(b). At Zero hour the Left Group Divisional Artillery will conform with the bombardment being carried out by the Division on our right by bombarding portions of the SWITCH LINE still in enemy hands.
Timings.:-
    Zero. ... 30 yds in front of objective.

Corrected by G127
d/ 14-8-16.

    0.30 ... Lift on to SWITCH LINE and remain there.

(c). Smoke discharge will commence at Zero along the whole front of the Division. Rate of discharge as detailed in paragraph 2 of 15th. Division Operation Order No. 75 of 15th. instant. It will continue till zero + 20 minutes.
During the discharge of smoke the line is to be thinly held. Lewis and machine guns to be active.
An Officer of the 4th. Company 5th. Battalion Special Brigade Royal Engineers will be present at the Headquarters of each Infantry Brigade from - 2 hours onwards to advise Brigades as to whether the wind is suitable or otherwise for the discharge of smoke.

(d). The Brigadier General Commanding 46th. Infantry Brigade will arrange to fire the pipes driven from LANCS SAP at an hour which he will arrange with the Left Brigade Right Division. The 46th. Infantry Brigade is to work in close co-operation with the Left Brigade of the Right Division and is to assist with machine gun and trench mortar fire.

(e)

Corrected by G.134
of 17/8/16.

(e). The correct signal time will be distributed by an Officer of the Corps Staff to representatives of Artillery and Infantry Brigades at Brigade Headquarters SHELTER WOOD at ~~12 noon~~ 11am on the 18th. instant.

(f). Zero time for this operation is not to be telephoned or wired.

H. Kent

Lieut. Colonel.
General Staff, 15th. Division.

Issued at 2 p.m.
to :-

III Corps.	Copies Nos. 1 & 2.
III Corps Arty.	Copy No. 3
III Corps H.A.	" " 4
1st. Division.	" " 5
1st. Australian Div.	" " 6
44th. Inf. Bde.	" " 7
45th. Inf. Bde.	" " 8
46th. Inf. Bde.	" " 9
9th. Gordons.	" " 10.
15th. Signals.	" " 11
15th. Div. Arty.	" " 12
34th. Div. Arty.	" " 13
47th. Div. Arty.	" " 14
C.R.E.	" " 15
A.D.M.S.	" " 16
A.P.M.	" " 17
"A" and "Q".	" " 18
War Diary.	" " 19
File.	" " 20
4th. Co.5th.Bn.Spec. Bde.R.E.	21

HEADQUARTERS
15th DIVISION.
17 AUG 1916
Reg. No. 1918

S E C R E T.   Copy No. 10

44th Infantry Brigade Operation Order No.78.

Reference :-   17-8-16.
15th Div.Map No.3.
d/14-8-16. 1/5,000.

1. On the 18th instant the Right Division is attacking, among other objectives, the INTERMEDIATE LINE from the road in S.2.d. to S.8.c.7.4.

2. The 15th Division will co-operate by the discharge of smoke on the Front S.2.c.5.7. to MUNSTER ALLEY for 20 minutes.

3. The discharge will be at the rate of :-
    1 "P" bomb for 25 yards per 2 minutes.
    4 candles for 25 yards per 1 minute.
   Number of bombs issued to Front Line Battalion for 500 yards front :-
    10 bombs for each of twenty 25-yard portions of Front Line Trench = 200.
   Number of candles issued to Front Line Battalion for 500 yards front :-
    80 candles for each of twenty 25-yard portions of Front Line Trench = 1600.

4. 4" Stokes Mortars will also assist.
   One Section of 4th Coy. 5th Battn. Special Brigade R.E. will be placed at the disposal of the Brigade to assist in arranging the smoke barrage.

5. Special bombardments of the objectives and of the SWITCH LINE East of S.1.4.8.8. will take place :-
    August 17th) 10 A.M. to 2 P.M.
    August 18th)

6. "Chinese" (see below) attacks will be made during above periods.
    ZERO times as follows :-
    August 17th) 1-30 P.M.
    August 18th)
   There will be five minutes intense fire from minus 5 minutes to ZERO. At ZERO the fire will lift. It will jump back suddenly at ZERO plus 90 seconds.
   Dummies, bayonets etc. will be exposed to lead the enemy to expect an attack when the barrage lifts and so induce him to line his parapets before the barrage drops back.
   The line to be lightly held during these special bombardments to avoid loss from enemy counter-barrage which may be expected during last portion of each period.
   If no dummies have been received sandbags on pickets will be used instead.

7. The 200 smoke bombs and 1600 smoke candles will be issued under arrangements to be made by Brigade Bomb Officer.

8. Watches will be synchronised at 9 A.M. on the 18th, at which hour a representative of :-
    The Front Line Battalion.
    Section 4th Coy. 5th Battn., Special Bde.R.E.
    The Support Battalion.
   will report at Brigade Headquarters.

                                      Major,
                                Brigade Major,   P. T. O.
                              44th Infantry Brigade.

Issued at 10-30 A.M.
Through Signals.

DISTRIBUTION.

Copy No. 1. 9th Black Watch.
2. 8th Seaforth Hrs.
3. 8/10th Gordon Hrs.
4. 7th Cameron Hrs.
5. 44th M.G.Coy.
6. 44th T.M.Battery.
7. Bde.Bombing Officer.
8. Staff Captain.
9. O.C.Section 4th Coy.5th Battn.;Spl.Bde.R.E.
10. 15th Division.
11. War Diary.

No 1945 G.S.

Signals 15th Div

Please detail

(a) An officer to
be at 44th Bde
H.Q at 6 a m
tomorrow
to synchronize
watches of
44th Bde & 23rd DA.

(b) An officer to
be present to
represent the
Div at synchronizing
of watches by
Corps at 46th
Bde H.Q. at
7 a m tomorrow.

Acknowledge.
P.T.O

H K
16/8/16

15th Division.

(a) Lt Ormsby.

(b) Lt Fox.

The above have been detailed.

[signature]
Capt RE
OC 15th Signal Coy

[signature]
16/8/16

"A" Form.   Army Form C. 2121.

MESSAGES AND SIGNALS. No. of Message_____

Prefix......Code......m	Words	Charge	This Message is on a/c of:	Recd. at......m
Office of Origin and Service Instructions. URGENT		HEADQUARTERS 15th DIVISION At......m To 16.AUG.1916 By...... (Signature of "Franking Officer.") Reg. No......	......Service.	Date...... From...... By......

TO { 15" Division

Sender's Number BM 688	Day of Month 16	In reply to Number	AAA

If the 1st Bde operation is successful tonight I am ordering the extension of 70" AVENUE to be continued to the ELBOW of the INTERMEDIATE TRENCH opposite LANES SAP, instead of forming NE to make a strong point. Please telephone if you concur

Replied GOC does not concur
9.45pm 16/6

From 46" 1 Bde
Place
Time 8.35pm

H. Mather
Bty ym

The above may be forwarded as now corrected. (Z)

....
Censor.   Signature of Addresser or person authorised to telegraph in his name.
° This line should be erased if not required.
T. & W. & J. M. Ltd., London. W 14042/M44. 75,000 12/15. Forms C 2121/10.

Headquarters,
15th Division.

The attached report on Bombing Attack by 10/11th High.L.I. on SWITCH LINE on 14.8.16., is forwarded.

(a) Report by O.C. 10/11 H.L.I.
(b) Statement by Cpl. Tweedie 73rd F.Coy R.E.

Brigade H.Q.
15.August, 1916.

T.S. Matheson
Brig.Gen.
Commanding,
46th Inf.Bde.

REPORT ON BOMBING ATTACK BY 10/11th
HIGH.L.I. on SWITCH LINE on 14.8.16.

By 10 a.m. all parties were in position.
Right Sap.
No 1 Party left the North end of Sap at zero time reaching
German line with very few casualties and Nos 1 and 2
parties bombed their ways East and West. No. 1 party which
was bombing East reached its objective very quickly and
the R.E. party which was following closely then created their
block. At this juncture bombs gave out as the men
had been throwing them unnecessarily. The Lewis Gun Team
had casualties before reaching enemy's parados; the
remaining two men fired the gun at the enemy who were
retiring over the open, until they were both knocked out.

No 2 party bombed their way along the Trench to the
West but owing to the lack of Support from the left Sap
party, which they were to meet, and bombs giving out as they
threw them unnecessarily and also because they met with strong
opposition they were unable to carry on and were eventually
forced to retire.

As far as I can gather some one in No 1 party shouted
the word "Retire" and the party came back to our Sap.

Left Sap. Parties were in position at zero hour.
Nos 1 and 2 parties left Sap as arranged in good order.
No 1 Party was met by heavy rifle or Machine Gun fire
and failed to effect an entry.

No 2 party got fairly clse up and found they could not get
in. The remaining parties never left the Sap owing to
Machine Gun fire. Enemy opened shell fire on SWITCH
LINE and Sap Head two minutes after commencement accompanied
by brisk rifle or Machine Gun fire. The O.C. Coy. finding
it impossible to get any men over the left Sap sent as many
men as he could collect to right Sap, but on their arrival
there the attack on the right had failed.

From the above collaborated report from O.C., Coys. and
what I have personally heard since I deduce that on the right
the attack was entirely successful and the position might have
been maintained if the two officers who were responsible for
this attack had not been knocked out at an early stage in the
proceedings. I understand that the right bombing party was in
the enemy's trench about one hour and this party which was met
by heavy opposition inflicted severe losses on the enemy
as did also the Lewis Gun before the last two men were knocked
out. I consider the failure of this party to be due to the
indiscriminate throwing of bombs and the Officer leading this
party being knocked out, and the Officer what was directing
the supply of men and bombs from the Sap, also being knocked
out.

A number of the enemy were seen to retire from their
Trench over the open and were accounted for by Lewis and
Machine Gun Fire.

Enemy trenches appear to be strongly held.

(Sgd) R. FORBES, Lt. Col.
Commanding, 10/11th High.L.I.

EVIDENCE OF R.E. WHO ACCOMPANIED 10/11th HIGH.L.I. IN ATTACK ON MORNING OF 14th Aug.

Cpl. TWEEDIE was in charge of a party of three sappers who went with the infantry attacking up the Right sap (i.e. continuation of WELCH ALLEY)

The R.E. followed "B" party ("A" and "B" parties being bombing parties). We formed up in the sap and the attack started at 10a.m. All the parties, "A", "B", and "C" went across hard on each other's heels. It was a run of quite 50 yards from head of sap to enemy's trench. I found the Infantry in front of me all in a cluster. the officer and his party had gone to the left. The others didn't appear to be going to move. They didn't appear to know what they were to do, so I called out to them "Get along, get along the bombers, to the right." They went to the right and the R.E. after them. We went along about 50 yards, when an Officer of the H.L.I. appeared on top of the parapet and took command of the bombers. We all went on to the right still further. past the light railway and about 20 yards beyond it. The officer then disappeared.

The trench had been well manned with Germans all of whom were killed as far as we went. These germans were all caught in little shelters scooped out in the front parapet and sides of traverses. I didn't see a single German in the trench itself. they were all in the shelters. I cannot state the number of dead Germans that I passed.

The trench was quite six feet below ground level, too much knocked about for me to state the width. no revetments, but the shelters were supported by semi-circular corrugated *iron sheets*. I cannot say how deep into the sides of the trench the shelters went.

When the Officer disappeared, as already stated, the bombers continued throwing bombs, and bombs were being thrown at them. I told them to hold on where they were, and we would form a block. They hung on and the R.E. formed a temporary block in the trench. I told the bombers to hold on there while I could get the wire to form the obstacle in the trench, and the second block. I couldn't find the wire, so I started the second (rearmost) block. The bombers at this time began to shout for more bombs, so I sent three of my working party to find bombs. A few minutes afterwards they passed up some bombs, but only in ones and twos - about half a dozen in all. By this time I had the block built up sufficiently for the inserting of my loophole frame. I passed the word along for this, but it couldn't be found (it was to have come up with the carrying party that was to have followed the attack later on) By this time we had run out of bombs and I called upon the Lewis gunner to get behind my block and cover the trench as the bombers were forced to come back. I then started to utilise sandbags to make a sandbag loophole, and having started my sappers on that I went off to the left to see the officer in charge of the left party of the right attack about bombs. I met him and asked him what he was going to do, so he went along to the right and I called for a volunteer to go back to fetch bombs: two men volunteered and set out. (Since the attack I have seen one of these two men. he had twisted his knee coming across and has now been sent to hospital; the other, when we returned later, I saw lying in the sap breathing his last).

I went along to the right then to where my party were at work. I found the Officer there and in command. A few seconds afterwards a bomb came and wounded the Lewis Gunner and I think it must have killed or knocked out the Officer (Lt. LEAN) for I never saw him again. Then having no bombs and no Lewis gunner I told my party of R.E. to stop work and come along to see if we could find any bombs. When we got back to the point where we had originally entered the trench, we saw the H.L.I. all on top rushing for the sap, so I ordered my party to come along quick too, and Sapper Jackson was the last man to leave the German trench. When retiring the rifle and machine gun fire was very hot, but there were very few shells.

On return to our trenches I reported to a Captain of H.L.I. who told me to make my party "stand by", which we did from about 11.20 a.m. to 3 p.m.

If we had had the bombs we would never have had to retire, but the carrying party never came over after us.

(Sgd) H.M.P. PALMER, Captain, R.E.

9th (Service) Battalion, Gordon Highlanders, (Pioneers).

16th August, 1916.

Headquarters,
   15th Division.

      Though the Company of Pioneers taking part in the operations North-east of CONTALMAISON on the night 12/13th August were not working under my orders I beg to report shortly as follows :-
1. The half company under orders of the 46th Infantry Brigade on the right was ordered to commence work at a definite time, i.e. 6 minutes past zero. Each platoon of this half company had to dig a trench previously begun by the explosion of a line of pipes driven to the front in the soil.
    (a) The right platoon was admirably commanded by a sergeant who would not allow them to leave the trench caused by the explosion as he realised that the assault had failed. This trench was easily dug out and the platoon returned to man the parapet suffering only two casualties.
    (b) The left platoon under 2nd Lieut. C. L. MacGregor worked under similar conditions but this officer attempted to trace the trench right up to the German line and was severely wounded.
2. The second half company, under 2nd Lieut. E. F. Harvie, working under the 45th Infantry Brigade on the left, was ordered not to advance until instructed to do so by the Officer Commanding right battalion - Royal Scots Fusiliers. On receipt of this order from Officer Commanding Royal Scots Fusiliers 2nd Lieut. Harvie led his men up a sap previously commenced in daylight and was wounded near the head of it, the assault on that part of the German line having failed. 2nd Lieut. Harvie as he was being brought in ordered his half company back to the front line and instructed his platoon sergeants to make no further attempt to dig the trench until they were sure the German line had been carried. About 12.30 a.m., under instructions from an Infantry Officer, two platoon sergeants again went out and were both wounded in an attempt to trace the trench, and finally a third sergeant was also wounded bringing them in. Captain MacMillan Commanding the company, who had remained with the Officer Commanding Royal Scots Fusiliers, as ordered by me, now arrived and, moving his two platoons 150 yards to the West and so opposite the part of the German trench that had been carried, dug the Boyau without loss or difficulty.

    The following points in foregoing report seem to merit consideration :-
1. The 46th Infantry Brigade gave a definite time for our work to commence. The 45th Infantry Brigade put the half company under the orders of a commanding officer. I prefer the former.
2. I only sent one officer with each half company and instructed the/

-2-

the Officer Commanding Company to remain in rear.   I should probably have lost more officers if I had allowed more to go.
3.   The pipes driven by the boring jack made quite a reasonable trench and saved many casualties.   One failed to explode with the electric exploder and fortunately my Sergeant made sure before going out.   It is reported that one explosion caused casualties to a Lewis Gun party.
4.   A sap partially dug in daylight towards a hostile trench is likely to have rifles trained on it.   I would rather break new ground.

................................Lt.-Col.,
Commanding 9th (Service) Battalion,
Gordon Highlanders, (Pioneers).

To,
General Staff,
    15th Division.

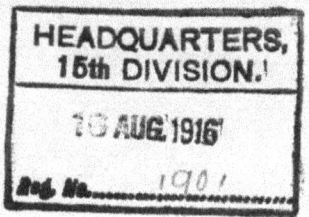

Reference attached, the 34th Divisional Artillery will all be busy box barraging 44th Infantry Attack.

Orders have been issued to Cancel Special Bombardment Table "B", in 34th Artillery Instructions No.50, at 10 a.m., and to continue under 34th Artillery Operation Order No.51 and orders from here.

                                        Major.
                            Brigade Major R.A.
17.8.1916.   34th Division.

To,
Headquarters,
47th Divisional Artillery.

Owing to Operations in O.O. No.51. the following alterations and additions are necessary to Artillery Instructions No.50.

At 9-30 a.m. turn Howitzers from work of Operation Order No.51. back to work of Table "A" Artillery Instructions No.50.

Howitzer Battery on Road S.2.a.5½.3½. to Road Elbow S.2.a.3.7. will however be kept on this objective till 10 a.m.

Reduce Rate of Fire of Table "A" to 30 rounds per hour for your Divisional Artillery.

At 10 a.m. to 2 p.m. Special Bombardment (Table B Arty. Instructions No.50).

<u>47th Divl.Arty.</u>   Bombard Switch Line S.1.d.8.9. to Road
   S.2.a.7.2. (inclusive).
<u>47th Divl.Arty.Hows.</u> (Less Table "A" Howitzers).
           Bombard Switch Line S.1.d.8.9. to
   S.2.a.50.0.5

No fire to be W of S.1.d.8.9.   Rates of Fire as in Artillery Instructions No.50.

Further Instructions will be issued re 'Chinese' Attack at 1-30 p.m.

         A. Main
         Major
         Brigade Major R.A.
         34th Division.

Copy to 15th Division.
       47th Divl.Arty.
       Diary.

SECRET.   Copy.No. 3

34TH DIVISIONAL ARTILLERY OPERATION ORDER NO.51.

Ref. 1/5000 Sheets.   16.8.1916.

1. On the 17th instant the 44th Infantry Brigade is attacking the German Switch Line from the ELBOW (S.1.d.4.8. westwards).

2. The 34th and 47th Divisional Artilleries will co-operate as follows:-
   (a) At Zero hour Barrage will be placed 20 yards in front of the German Switch Line from S.2.a.9.4. to X.6.a.9.3.
   (b) At Zero hour fire will also be opened on suspected Machine Guns in area S.1.d.5.7. to S.1.d.4.7.
   (c) At Zero+1' the Barrage in (a) W of S.1.d.5.8. will lift 120 yards.
   (d) At Zero+2' the Artillery firing on area in (b) will lift 200 yards.
   (e) Heavy Artillery are co-operating on various points in rear. Time Table for 34th and 47th Divl.Artilleries attached.

3. Zero hour 8-55 a.m.

4. 34th and 47th Divisional Artilleries will synchronise Watches at 44th Infantry Brigade Headquarters at CONTALMAISON at 6 a.m. on August 17th.
   O.C.Brigades 34th Divisional Artillery will send a representative from each Brigade to CONTALMAISON at 6 a.m. for this purpose.

5. Acknowledge.

Issued at 8-15 p.m.
   Copy No.1. R.A.IIIrd Corps.
        2. IIIrd Corps Hy.Arty.
        3. 15th Division.
        4. 47th Divl.Arty.
        5. 1st Divl.Arty.
        6. Lahore Arty.
        7. 152nd F.A.Bdes.
        8. 160th -do-
        9. 175th -do-
       10. 176th -do-
    11-13 Diary.

                                            Major
                                      Brigade Major R.A.
                                         34th Division.

SECRET.

TIME TABLE TO ACCOMPANY 34TH DIVISIONAL ARTILLERY OPERATION ORDER
No. 51

(1) <u>0. to 0.1.</u> <u>152nd F.A.Brigade.</u> 2 18-pdr.Batteries.
Barrage Tramline R.36.c.4.0. to M.31.d.5.5.
<u>160th F.A.Brigade.</u> 3 18-pdr.Batteries.
Search Trenches S.1.b.5½.4. to M.31.d.8.3.
                    1 Howitzer Battery.
Trench M.31.d.7½.5. to M.31.d.9.2½.
<u>175th F.A.Brigade.</u> 3 18-pdr.Batteries.
Barrage 20 yards in front of German Switch Line
from X.6.a.9.3. to S.1.b.1.0.
(Note:- Our Troops are at X.6.a.7¼.2½.)
                    1 Howitzer Battery.
On Tramline M.31.d.5.5. to M.31.d.9.6½.
<u>176th F.A.Brigade.</u> 3 18-pdr.Batteries.
Barrage 20 yards in front of German Switch Line
from S.1.b.1.0. to S.1.d.5.8.
                    1 Howitzer Battery.
On Tramline M.31.d.5.5. to M.31.d.9.6½.

<u>47th Divl.Artillery.</u> Double Barrage on German
Switch Line S.1.d.5.8. to S.2.a.9.3. with
18-pdr.Batteries of three F.A.Brigades(less
1 Battery), and one Howitzer Battery. Front
Line of Barrage to be 20 yards in front of
German Switch Line.
<u>1 Brigade 18-pdrs.</u> On Trench M.31.d.9.2½. to
S.2.a.4.9.
<u>1 Howitzer Battery.</u> On Road X.2.a.5½.3½. to
Road Elbow S.2.a.3.7.
1 Howitzer Battery on Tramline Triangle in
M.32.c. and along Tramline to M.31.d.9.8.

*At O to O.2
1 Bty 47th Div. Arty
on suspected Machine
Guns in area
S.1.d 5.7 - S.1 d 4.7 →*

(2) <u>At 0.1.</u> <u>152nd F.A.Brigade.</u> 1 Battery continue Barrage
R.36.c.8.2. to M.31.d.5.5. Remaining Battery
Barrage R.36.c.6.1. to S.1.b.6.0. and search to
N.E. of this.
<u>175th F.A.Bde. 18-pdrs.</u> Lift 120 yards.
<u>176th F.A.Bde. 18-pdrs.</u> Lift 120 yards.
Remainder as at Zero.

(3) <u>At 0.2.</u> The Battery of 47th Divl.Artillery on Area
S.1.d.5.7. to S.1.d.4.7. lifts 200 yards.

Fire will be continued till further Orders.

<u>Rates of fire:-</u>
0. to 0.5. 3 Rounds per Gun per Minute.
0.5. to 0.15. 2 Rounds per Gun per minute.
0.15 onwards. 1 round per Gun per Minute.
The rear portion of 47th Divl.Artillery double Barrage will
search and sweep.

"A" Form. Army Form C. 2121.
MESSAGES AND SIGNALS. No. of Message _____

TO: 15th DIV

17 AUG 1916

Sender's Number: BM 711
Day of Month: 17th
AAA

Barrel Jack in LANCS SAP was in process of being set up at 7 am RE Officer in charge expects to have plant ready for boring on a short. Infantry party were standing by to assist in pumping and passing up material.

From: 46.113
Time: 8.30 am

"A" Form. — MESSAGES AND SIGNALS. Army Form C. 2121.

TO: 15th Division

Stamp: HEADQUARTERS 15th DIVISION — 17 AUG 1916 — Reg. No. 1907

Sender's Number: BM 709
Day of Month: 17
AAA

H21 Trench extended about another 30 yards practically completely dug to that point AAA 70 AVENUE only improved up to point it was dug to yesterday AAA It is regretted it was quite impossible to work in open last night owing to heavy artillery fire in that vicinity. RE officer was unable to mark out extension of Trench owing to this. Have ordered sapping to commence in new direction after 2 pm today AAA PIONEER TRENCH 80 yds long connect with LANES TRENCH and 70° AVENUE should be completed in a few hours

From: 46th Bde

Signature: J. W. Bash Capt. for Brig Gen

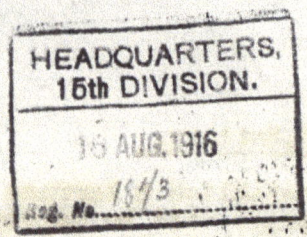

HEADQUARTERS,
15th DIVISION.
16 AUG.1916
Reg. No. 18/3

S E C R E T.   COPY No. 7

44th Infantry Brigade Operation Order No.75.

16-8-16.

Reference.
15th Divn.Map No.3
 d/14-8-16. 1/5000.

1. 44th Infantry Brigade will attack German trench line between the points S.1.d.4.8. and X.6.a.7.3. on 17th instant at an hour to be notified later.

2. 7th Cameron Hrs. will find the assaulting party.

    III Corps H.A., 34th Div.Arty., 46th T.M.Battery and 46th M.G.Coy. will co-operate as indicated below.-

3.(a) Action by 7th Cameron Hrs.
   (i) Dig a trench parallel to German line at a distance of about 100 yards from it, running from GLOSTER Alley to Boyau joining BUTTERWORTH Trench and New Switch. Work to be completed by 6 A.M. 17th.

   (ii) Assaulting party to be in position in this trench half-hour before "ZERO" hour, organised as covering party with Lewis guns, clearing party and digging party.

   (iii) At "ZERO" hour to rush German trench.

   (iv) (a) The covering party will push on as far as our barrage permits.
   (b) The clearing party will clear trenches and establish double blocks at about S.1.d.4.8. and X.6.a.9.3.(if necessary).
   (c) The digging party will commence the construction of strong points at about S.1.b.0.3. S.1.b.1.1. X.6.a.9.3. A special party will be detailed to join GLOSTER Sap to the German line.
   O.C.73rd Fld.Coy.R.E. will detail parties to supervise and assist in the construction of strong points and blocks.
   Wire for wiring the strong points will be collected under Brigade arrangements at junctions of Boyaux and new trench mentioned in para 3.(a) (i).
   (v) As soon as the trench has been cleared of Germans, all men not required for covering, digging, or holding the trench, will be withdrawn into our original lines.
   (vi) Dress. Fighting order. Sufficient food and water for 24 hours will be carried.

(b) Action by 9th Black Watch.
   (i) Clear GLOSTER Alley and BUTTERWORTH Trench, up to Boyau leading to New Switch, of troops by 7 A.M.
   (ii) Detail a party to connect point X.6.a.8.2. to German line about X.6.a.9.3.
   This party will be ready to commence work as soon as the German trench has been carried.

(1.)   P.T.O.

(c). **Action by 44th T.M.Battery.**

(i) At "ZERO" hour establish a barrage on German trench about S.1.d.5.8. This barrage will be maintained until O.C.7th Cameron Hrs. decides that it is no longer necessary.
(ii) At "ZERO" hour establish an intense bombardment of German trench from about X.6.a.9.1½ to a.9.3. This bombardment will cease when the Artillery barrage lifts.

46th T.M.Battery will co-operate at zero hour by bombarding German line from point S.1.d.5.8. Eastwards to railway. Bombardment to continue to + 15 minutes.

(d) **Action by 44th M.G.Coy.**

(i) To cover the flank of the attack from Point X.6.a.0.5. to the east, and to be ready to take advantage of all targets which may present themselves.
(ii) To keep down hostile fire which may come from snipers in shell holes east of GLOSTER Alley, and S.of German trench.

46th M.G.Coy. will co-operate to the east.

4. In the event of the Reserve Coy. of 7th Cameron Hrs. being drawn into the fight, 9th Black Watch will re-occupy the trenches vacated by them.

5. 8th Seaforth Hrs. will move 2 Companies to GOURLAY Trench from which two platoons will be detailed to be ready to carry bombs and S.A.A. from CONTALMAISON VILLA to BUTTERWORTH Trench.
H.Qrs. and 2 Companies to CONTALMAISON. Move to be complete by 7 A.M. 17th instant.

6. Prisoners will be sent to Collecting Station at X.28.b.2.6.

7. **Outline of Artillery action.**   34th Divisional Artillery.

(i) At zero hour open an intense barrage 20 yards in front German trench from S.2.a.9.4. to X.6.a.9.3.
(ii) At plus 1 minute to lift on front of attack to 120 yards and forming a box round area being consolidated.

(iii) Maintain barrage on rest of German line.

(iv) Deal with dangerous points in area.

Corps Artillery.
Shell road cutting in S.2.a., MARTINPUICH, strong points about X.6.a.2.9. and R.35.b.4.4. with H.A. and gas shells.

Deal with dangerous points in area.

Issued Through
Signals. 130 P.M.

Caberk. Major,
Brigade Major,
44th Infantry Brigade.

Copy No. 1. 9th Black Watch.   10. 15th Div.Arty.
         2. 8th Seaforth Hrs.   11. 34th Div.Arty.
         3. 8/10th Gordon Hrs.   12. 73rd Fld.Coy.R.E.
         4. 7th Cameron Hrs.   13. 45th Fld.Amb.
         5. 44th M.G.Coy.   14. Bde.Signal Section.
         6. 44th T.M.Battery.   15. 9th Gordons (Pioneers).
         7. 15th Div.   16. Staff Captain.
         8. 46th Inf.Bde.   17. War Diary.
         9. 4th Aust. Inf.Bde.   18. File.

SECRET   Copy No 12

46th Infantry Brigade Order No 86.

16.8.16.

1. On 17th inst. the 44th Infantry Brigade will attack the SWITCH LINE from the ELBOW westwards and connect it up with GLOSTER SAP and with our front line about X.6.a.7.3.

2. Zero time will be communicated later.

3. To assist in this operation 46th Infantry Brigade will cover the attack of 44th Infantry Brigade with Machine Guns, Lewis Guns and Trench Mortars.

4. O.C., 46th Machine Gun Company and O.C. 46th Trench Mortar Battery will act in accordance with instructions received from G.O.C., 44th Infantry Brigade to whom they will report.

5. Machine Guns, Lewis Guns and Trench Mortars will be specially on the alert to pick up targets and immediately bring fire to bear on any of the enemy who may leave their trenches.

6. During our heavy bombardment troops in the Front system will take cover as far as possible, but Machine and Lewis Gunners and Trench Mortars are to stand by to watch for targets.

7. (a) An intense barrage will open 20 yds in front of the whole German SWITCH LINE from S.2.a.9.4. to X.6.a.9.3. at zero.

   (b) This barrage at O. plus 1 minute will lift 120 yds. on the front S.1.d.5.8. to X.6.a.9.3., the remainder of the barrage will not lift.
It will not lift till O. plus 2 minutes between H.L.I. trench and SWITCH ELBOW.

   (c) The Artillery fire will be maintained at varying intensity and as found necessary till the position is consolidated.

   (d) Gas shells will be fired on various positions in rear.

   (e) Heavy artillery will fire on objectives to be selected.

   (f) During the artillery barrage troops in the front system will take cover as far as possible but Machine and Lewis Gunners and Trench Mortar Batteries are to stand by and watch for targets. H.L.I. trench must be cleared to the N.W. of a point 50 yds from LANCS TRENCH.

8. Work on the new Trench (H.L.I. Trench) towards the ELBOW is to be pushed on as quickly as possible by sapping, under supervision of O.C., Left Sub-section.

9. This will be a separate operation to the bombardment mentioned in Para 4 of B.M./6/4 dated 16th inst. which must not be forgotten.

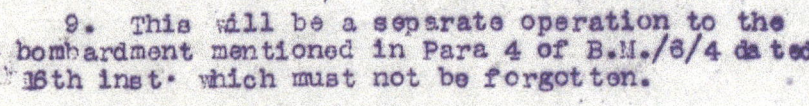

2.

10. All reference to this operation on the
telephone is to be avoided, on no account are times
to be mentioned in clear

                                    Captain,
                                       Bde Maj.,
                                       46th Inf.Bde.

Issued at
    through Signals.

Copy No	
1	File
2	War Diary
3	7/8th K.O.Sco.Bord.
4	10th Sco.Rif;
5	10/11th High.L.I.
6	12th High.L.I.
7	46th M.G. Coy.
8	46th T.M.Battery
9	73rd Field Coy. R.E.
10	Medium T.M.Battery
11	44th Inf. Bde.
12	15th Division.

46th Inf. Bde.
No. B.M/48/9

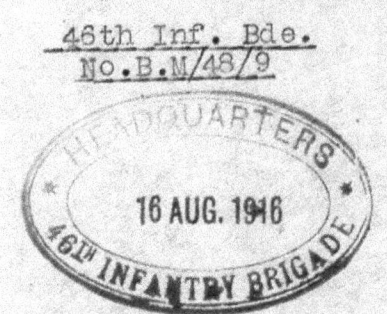

Headquarters,
    15th Division.

Reference 15th Division No. 100(1)/4.G.a. dated 13th instant, para.2.

I doubt whether, when the continuation of 70th AVENUE is complete, it will be possible to bring reverse fire to bear on the INTERMEDIATE LINE because there appears to be high broken ground on the west side of the road which will defilade the INTERMEDIATE LINE from view.

Brig. Gen.,
Commanding,
46th Inf. Bde.

Brigade Headquarters,
    16 August, 1916.

Urgent

46th Inf. Bde.
No. B.M/1/55

HEADQUARTERS
16 AUG. 1916
46TH INFANTRY BRIGADE

Headquarters,
15th Division.

Reference 15th Division O.O. No. 73 dated 15th inst., para. 3 (a).

If the deliberate bombardment which begins at 5 p.m. to-day on the INTERMEDIATE LINE lasts till ZERO on the 18th inst., it appears to me that I possibly may not be able to work at the Barret Jack in LANCS TRENCH or continue extension of 70th AVENUE after 5 p.m. to-day.

Will you please instruct me as to which trenches should be kept clear during the whole of this period.

T.J. Matthew
Brig. Gen.,
Commanding,
46th Inf. Bde.

Brigade H.Q.
August, 1916.

SECRET.

15th. Division
No.100/4 G.a.

III Corps.	C.R.E.	
III Corps Arty.	9th. Gordons.	
III Corps H.A.	44th. Inf. Bde.)	Reference 15th.Div.
34th. Div. Arty.	45th. Inf. Bde.)	No.100/4 G.a. dated
47th. Div. Arty.	46th. Inf. Bde.)	15th. August 1916.
1st. Division.		
1st. Australian Div.		

----

1. On the 17th. instant the 44th. Infantry Brigade is attacking the German SWITCH LINE from the ELBOW (S.1.d.4.8) westwards.

  (a). At zero hour a barrage will be placed 20 yards in front of the German SWITCH LINE from S.2.a.9.4 to X.6.a.9.3.

  (b). At zero hour Artillery will also open on suspected machine guns in the Area S.1.d.5.7 to S.1.d.4.7.

  (c). At zero $+$ 1 the barrage in (a) above westward of S.1.d.5.8 will lift 120 yards.

  (d). At zero $+$ 2 minutes the Artillery firing on area in (b) above will lift.

  (e). Heavy Artillery are co-operating on various points in rear.

2. It has been arranged with the III Corps that on the 17th. during the bombardment which commences at 10 a.m (15th. Div. O.O. 75 and III Corps O.O.110 Addendum No.I) no heavy Artillery is to fire on the SWITCH LINE west of S.1.d.8.9 but Heavy Artillery will fire after 10 a.m on the SWITCH LINE east of S.1.d.8.9.

x Not issued to units of 15" Div

3. Zero hour for the operation mentioned in paragraph 1 above will be 8.55 a.m. 17th. August.
  Watches of Infantry Brigades and 34th. Div. Artillery will be synchronized at 44th. Infantry Brigade Headquarters CONTALMAISON at 6 a.m. on August 17th.

4. ACKNOWLEDGE. *(Not to units outside Div. control)*

H. Knox
Lieut. Colonel.
General Staff, 15th. Division.

4 p.m.
16th. August 1916.

"A" Form.   Army Form C. 2121.
MESSAGES AND SIGNALS.   No. of Message

Prefix	Code	m	Words	Charge	This message is on a/c of:	Recd. at .... m
Office of Origin and Service Instructions.			Sent			Date
			At .... m		Service.	From
			To			
			By		(Signature of "Franking Officer.")	By

TO   A R

* G47   Day of Month 15-Aug   In reply to Number   A A A

Your BN 793 17/7/7 GOC does
not approve

From Q13
Place
Time 2-20 pm

(Z) K Henderson Major Gd

HEADQUARTERS,
15th DIVISION.
15 AUG 1916
Reg. No. 1854

SECRET

44th Brigade.

H.Q., 15th Division.

Proposed Operation by 44th Infantry Brigade, 15/8/16.

Reference attached plan.

A., B., and C. to D. are held by Germans.

At 4 P.M. 2 platoons will attack from GLOSTER ALLEY and 2 from trench that runs from BUTTERWORTH Trench to Pt.X.

Special parties will attack A. and B. from X.

Support platoons, 2 in GLOSTER ALLEY,
4 in BUTTERWORTH Tr. to X.
2 in BUTTERWORTH Trench. (found by "B" Battn.)

Reserve. 1 Coy. "B" Battn. from CONTALMAISON to GOURLAY Trench.

Lewis Guns told off to occupy captured trench.

"A" Battn. Pioneers to connect GLOSTER SAP with SWITCH. Post held by 8/10th Gordons is now being joined to front line.

Stokes guns will barrage D. at 4-2 P.M.

Artillery. At 4-5 P.M. a light barrage from X.6.a.3.10. to S.1.b.9½.5.

Road cutting in S.2.a.3.6. to be dealt with by H.AM.

46th Brigade to bombard SWITCH with Stokes from D. eastward as soon as 44th T.M.Battery opens, and also deal with enemy leaving SWITCH opposite 46th Brigade.

Detailed arrangements have been made by O.C.8/10th Gordons with his Company Commanders (G.O.C.Brigade was present at the conference).

May approval or the reverse be notified by telephone, please.

Brigadier General,
Commdg. 44th Infantry Brigade.

15-8-16.

15TH DIVISION MAP N° 3.
14/8/16   1:5,000.

R   35   36   31

held by 8/10 Gordons.
A
B
C
D

Vickers
Vickers

TORR TR.
MUNSTER
ALLEY
THE LOOP
PITHIE POST
New C.T. (Gordons)
BUTTERWORTH TR.
6TH AVENUE
GLOSTER ALLEY
Vickers
Stokes
Stokes
Stokes
LANCS TR.
6TH AVENUE
BLACK WATCH ALLEY.
WELCH ALLEY.

Copy No.____

15th. Division Operation Order No.75.

Reference :-
   Sheets 57^D SE & 57^C SW.
   ----------1/20,000.--------

Headquarters,
15th. Division.
15th. August 1916.

1. On the 18th. instant the Right Division is attacking among other objectives the INTERMEDIATE LINE from the road in S.2.d. to S.2.c.7.4.
   Certain steps in preparation for the above have been ordered in 15th. Division No.100(1)/4 G.a. dated 13th. August 1916.

2. The 15th. Division will co-operate on the 18th. instant by the discharge of smoke on the front S.2.c.3.7. to MUNSTER ALLEY for twenty minutes.
   The discharge will be at the rate of :-
      one P bomb for 25 yds per two minutes.
      four candles for 25 yds per one minute.
   4" Stokes mortars will also assist.
   One Section of the 4th. company 5th. Battalion Special Brigade R.E. will be placed at the disposal of each Brigade in line to assist in arranging the smoke barrage.

3. In preparation for the above operation :-
   (a). There will be a deliberate bombardment of the objective commencing at 5 p.m. August 16th. and continuing till Zero on the 18th.

   (b). Special bombardments of the objective and of the SWITCH LINE will take place :-
      August 16th. ... 5 p.m. to 8 p.m.
      August 17th.)
      August 18th.) ... 10 a.m to 2 p.m.
      Details will be issued later.
   During these special bombardments all trenches and saps within 200 yds of the target will be cleared and re-occupied immediately after the bombardment is over, viz:- at 8 p.m. and 2 p.m. respectively.
   The front to be covered by machine guns.

   (c). "Chinese" (see below) attacks will be made during above periods; Zero times as follows :-
      August 16th. ... 7.30 p.m.
      August 17th.)
      August 18th.) ... 1.30 p.m.
   There will be five minutes intense fire from minus 5 minutes to Zero. At Zero the fire will lift. It will jump back suddenly at Zero plus 90 seconds.
   Dummies, bayonets etc. etc. will be exposed to lead the enemy to expect an attack when the barrage lifts and so induce him to line his parapets before the barrage drops back.
   The line to be lightly held during these special bombardments to avoid loss from the enemy counter-barrage which may be expected during the last portion of each period.

4. Signal time will be distributed by an Officer of the Corps Staff at Brigade Headquarters, SHELTER WOOD, at 2 p.m. on 16th. and 7 a.m. on 17th. and 18th. Representatives of Artillery and Infantry Brigades to be present.

H. Knox

Lieut. Colonel.

<u>General Staff, 15th. Division.</u>

Issued at 9 p.m.
to :-

III Corps.	Copies Nos.	1&2.
III Corps Artillery.	Copy No.	3.
III Corps H. Arty...	"	4.
1st. Division.	"	5.
4th. Australian Div.	"	6.
44th. Inf. Bde.	"	7.
45th. Inf. Bde.	"	8.
46th. Inf. Bde.	"	9.
9th. Gordons.	"	10.
15th. Signals.	"	11.
15th. Div. Arty.	"	12.
34th. Div. Arty.	"	13.
47th. Div. Arty.	"	14.
C.R.E.	"	15.
A.D.M.S.	"	16.
A.P.M.	"	17.
"A" & "Q".	"	18.
War Diary.	"	19.
File.	"	20.

(Copy)

SECRET.
15th. Div.
No.100(1)/4 G.a.

44th. Inf. Bde.
45th. Inf. Bde.
46th. Inf. Bde.
34th. Div. Artillery.

X

Reference 15th.Div. No.100/4 G.a. dated 15.8.16.

+ Copy sent to III Corps

1. The Corps Commander has approved of the proposals with the modification that the barrage should lift 120 yds not 220 yds.

2. During the bombardment which will commence at 5 p.m. tomorrow, the Heavy Artillery will obliterate the SWITCH LINE between S.1.d.4.8 (80 yards east of GLOSTER ALLEY) for some distance ~~westwards~~ Eastwards.
 The gap so formed to be kept open by Trench mortar and machine gun fire.

H. Knox
Lieut. Colonel
15th. August 1916.   General Staff, 15th. Division.

Copy to :-
 III Corps
  for information.

S E C R E T.
15th Division No. 150/4 G.a.

44th Inf. Bde.
45th Inf. Bde.
46th Inf. Bde.
34th D.A.
----

1. At a conference held this afternoon at the 46th Bde. Hd. Qrs. to discuss further operations against the SWITCH LINE it was decided :-

(i). The 46th Inf. Bde. to push on work on the sap designed to connect LANCS TRENCH with the SWITCH LINE.

(ii). The 46th Inf. Bde. to assist the 44th Inf. Bde. by covering their attack with trench mortar and machine gun fire.

(iii). The 44th Inf. Bde. to attack the SWITCH from the ELBOW Westwards and to connect it up with GLOSTER SAP and with our present front line about X.6.a.7.3.
    Date to be 17th August. Zero time to be fixed later.

(iv). In preparation for this attack the 44th Inf. Bde. to prepare a jumping off line by connecting the cut from GLOSTER SAP to the New Trench about X.6.a.7.2. and so to form a line parallel with front to be attacked.
    A pusher to be installed at end of GLOSTER SAP.

(v). The attack to be carried out by 2 companies (or more if desired).
    Blocking parties for right and for left (new cut northwards from German SWITCH) to be organized.
    Consolidation parties to be detailed. Too many men not to be kept on the position once it is captured. Infantry to attack close under the barrage.
    The B.G.C. 44th. Inf. Bde. to prepare his plan and submit it for the approval of the G.O.C. as soon as possible.

(vi) <u>Artillery support</u> :-

(a). An intense barrage to open 20 yds in front of whole German SWITCH LINE from S.2.a.9.4. to X.6.a.9.3. at zero.
    This barrage at 0+1 mins to lift 220 yds on the front S.1.d.5.8 to X.6.a.9.3. The remainder of the barrage not to lift.
    Artillery fire to be maintained at varying intensity and as found necessary till the position is consolidated.

(b). Gas shells to be fired on various positions in rear.

(c). Heavy Artillery on certain objectives to be selected.

(d). A practice barrage as in (a) above xxxxxxxxxxxxxxxxx xxxxxxxxx but lifting along whole line after 1 minute and dropping back again will be carried out at 4 p.m. on the 16th. instant. (<u>Brigades in line will be prepared accordingly</u>)

2. The G.O.C. wishes all reference to this operation on the telephone to be avoided. On no account are times to be mentioned in clear.

                                                    Lieut. Colonel.

15th. August 1916.   General Staff, 15th. Division.

SECRET   Copy No 13

                    46th Infantry Brigade Order No 85

                                                          13/8/16

HEADQUARTERS.
15th DIVISION.
  AUG. 1916
Reg. No.........

1. The 10/11th High.L.I. will, under instructions which have already been communicated to him verbally, make a bombing attack to-morrow on the SWITCH LINE opposite the saps already made by the Boring Jack.

2. The hour "zero" will be communicated later.

3. O.C., Machine Gun Company and O.C., Trench Mortar Battery will be placed under orders of O.C., 10/11th High.L.I., for the operations, to whom they will report at 8 a.m.

4. O.C., 10/11th High.L.I. will make his own arrangements for the supply of bombs, S.A.A., tools, sandbags, wiring material, etc. He will apply to Brigade Headquarters before 6 a.m. to-morrow for any special assistance he may require.

5. There will be no special Artillery preparations.

6. Two stops will be created in the GERMAN SWITCH 40 yards apart, to the east of the right hand Sap, two others will be created to the west of the left hand Sap if it is not possible to get touch with the Left Brigade.

(ack)
two on

7. O.C., 73rd Field Coy. R.E. will detail two parties, each consisting of 1 N.C.O. and 3 men to work at the back stop of each double stop.

8. The two companies, 7/8th K.O.Sco.Bord. in the cutting will stand to arms ready to move at a moments notice from zero hour until dismissed.

                                        Captain,
                                        Bde Maj.,
                                        46th Inf.Bde.

Issued at 8.30
    through Signals.

                    Copy No 1. 7/8th K.O.Sco.Bord.
                           2.   10th Sco.Rif.
                           3.   10/11th High.L.I.
                           4.   12th High.L.I.
                           5.   46th Trench Mortar Battery
                           6.   46th Machine Gun Coy.
                           7.   Brigade Signals
                           8.   Staff Captain
                           9.   73rd Field Coy. R.E.
                           10. 44th Inf. Bde.
                           11. 45th Inf. Bde.
                           12. 112th Inf. Bde.
                           13. 15th Division
                           14. Spare
                           15. Spare

23rd DA
To see
K Henderson Major GS
14/8/16

Seen + returned
ack

S E C R E T.

URGENT.   15th Div. No. 100(2)/4 G.a.

III Corps H. Arty.
_____

    With reference to the small operation being carried out by 46th Inf. Bde. tomorrow, herewith copy of letter sent to III Corps and III Corps Artillery.

                                        Lieut. Colonel,
12th Aug.1916.   General Staff, 15th Division.

"C" Form (Original).   Army Form C. 2123.
MESSAGES AND SIGNALS.   No. of Message..........

Prefix....... Code.... Words..22. Received From.......... Sent, or sent out At.......m. Office Stamp.
Charges to collect £ s. d. By.. Gale To..........
Service Instructions. Priority   By..........

Handed in at...3Ca............ Office 11.35 m. Received 12.0 m.

TO   15th Division

| *Sender's Number | Day of Month | In reply to Number | AAA |
| G.19 | 13th | 100(2)/4 GR | |

Approved and arrange wire paragraph 2 direct with 3rd Corps Heavy Artillery

12.14 a.m

FROM PLACE & TIME   3rd Corps 11.50 pm

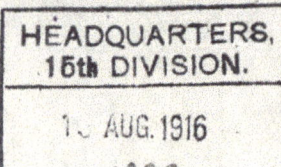

HEADQUARTERS,
15th DIVISION.
1... AUG. 1916
Reg. No. 1630

S E C R E T.   46th Inf. Bde.
                                                                No. G/1/92.

O.C.
     Bde. Signals.
     Staff Captain.
     73rd Field Coy. R.E.
     44th Inf. Bde.
     45th Inf. Bde.
     112th Inf. Bde.
     15th Division.
     File.
     War Diary.

         Reference 46th Infantry Brigade Order No.85 para 2 dated 13th instant,

            ZERO = 10 a.m.

Brigade Headquarters,   Captain,
      13th August, 1916.   Bde. Major,
                                                                         46th Inf. Bde.

SECRET.

46th Inf. Bde.
No. O/1/91.

Headquarters,
15th Division.
----

1. With reference to 15th Division O.O. No.74, I propose to deal with the situation in the following manner.

(a) To extend saps and "A" and "B", as shown dotted on attached plan, with all possible speed towards the SWITCH LINE. These saps are now being pushed on and should be completed nearly to the SWITCH LINE before daylight.

(b) On the morning of the 14th instant probably at 10 a.m. a bombing attack will be made down sap "A" bombing squads rushing into the SWITCH LINE at point "C". One squad to establish a block at "X". The remaining squads to work westwards along SWITCH LINE towards "Z".

(c) As soon as block at "X" is established and other squads have worked westwards any portion of A C not dug will be cleared working from both ends.

(d) A similar bombing attack will work down Sap "B" establish a block at "Z" and if necessary working Eastwards towards "C" and join up any portion of B Z not completed.

(e) This being complete it is proposed to work West towards the ELBOW and get touch with left Inf. Bde.

2. I do not propose to carry out the instructions in para 2 of the Operation Order referred to so far as pushing out the trench from LANCS TRENCH to join the SWITCH ELBOW unless the operation proves impossible.

3. Trench Mortars and Machine Guns in Sub-section will be at the disposal of O.C., 10/11th High.L.I. who will carry out the whole operation. These will probably not be used except in case of obstinate resistance.

4. No special Artillery co-operation is asked for but the usual barrages may continue towards MARTINPUICH but should not come within 250 yds of the area being operated on. The junction of INTERMEDIATE LINE with German SWITCH LINE at S.2.a.6.1. might with advantage receive special attention.

5. G.O.C., 45th Infantry Brigade states he requires no particular co-operation this evening when he is carrying out a small operation at the elbow.

Brigade Headquarters,
13 August, 1916.

Brig.Gen.
Commanding,
46th Inf.Bde.

SECRET.

15th Division No. 100(2)/4 G.s.

III Corps.
III Corps Artillery.
----

1. I have approved of an attack being made tomorrow at 10 a.m. (approximately) on the German SWITCH LINE in S.1.d.
The plan is briefly as follows :-

   (i). Saps A and B are being pushed out tonight to close to SWITCH LINE.

   (ii). Bomb attack from A and block trench at X.

   (iii). Ditto from B and block at Z.

   (iv). Connect with Left.Bde.

   (v). Necessary artillery has been arranged.

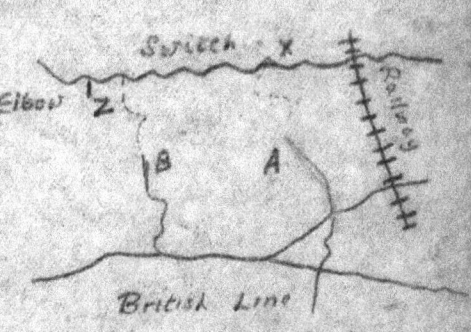

2. When this attack is over, say after 11 a.m. or later if necessary, I should be glad if heavy artillery could deal with SWITCH LINE east of Railway.
If the attack is unsuccessful I will arrange to vacate the necessary trenches to enable the H.A. to deal with the SWITCH from ELBOW eastwards, i.e., all trenches within 300 yards to be vacated.

Major General,

13th Aug.,1916.   Commanding, 15th (Scottish) Division.

2.

46th Inf. Bde.

(i). Presumably you have arranged with Left Bde. to cover your operation with machine gun fire?

(ii). You will be informed in due course when H.A. propose to shoot.

Lieut. Colonel,

13-8-16.   General Staff,15th Division.

3.

23rd D.A.

For information.

Lieut. Colonel,

13-8-16.   G.s. 15th Div.

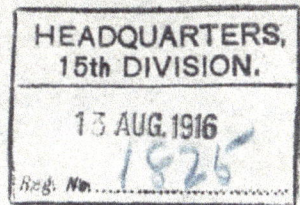

HEADQUARTERS,
15th DIVISION.

13 AUG. 1916

Reg. No. 1825

46th Inf. Bde.
No.B.M/1/47.

Headquarters,
   15th Division.

OPERATION REPORT.

   1. From reports received from my Right Battalion, 10th Sco. Rif., it seems clear that the enemy attacked near LANCS SAP about 10.25 p.m. last night. This attack was repulsed after a stiff bombing contest. It is thought that this attack was covered by enfilade fire along 70th AVENUE from which the 12th High.L.I. suffered so heavily when they were getting in position and whilst in position for the assault on the GERMAN SWITCH LINE.

   2. O.C., 12th High.L.I. informs me that as his Battalion was getting into position outside our front parapet from 10 p.m. onwards it was subjected to heavy Machine gun fire both from the East and from the N.W. An officer who was on the left of the Battalion - 2nd Lieut. BRYAN - has made a report that he saw what appeared to be an observation or Machine Gun position in a shell hole to his left front in advance of the German Line about 120 yards from our Line. Machine gun fire appears to have come from this direction.

   3. As far as I can ascertain the advance was begun at 10.30 p.m. but after going 40 yards or so it was held up by machine gun fire. Some may have got further, but as all the Officers were either killed or wounded it is very difficult to get reliable information.

   4. The officers of the Right Company appear to have become casualties early, and it is reported that the Right Company deviated slightly from its correct direction and then withdrew but afterwards advanced again, but only for about 50 yards at the most.

   5. It seemed quite impossible to get through the Machine Gun fire and ultimately the 3 attacking Companies, or what remained of them, withdrew on our original front line.

   6. The casualties, I am informed, amounted to 15 Officers and about 300 Other Ranks, but I think this is probably an overestimation.

   7. The information I first received led me to imagine that the operation was successful as it was reported that there were no Very lights going up and little Machine gun fire. However, later it was reported to me that enemy Very lights went up about 10.50 p.m. along the whole line and machine guns opened fire.

   8. No definite news could be obtained till 11.30 p.m., all Officers being killed or wounded by that time and from an inspection of the front line about 11.15 p.m. the attacking troops appeared to be still out.

   9. When I heard the attacking Companies were held up about 12.19 a.m., I ordered O.C., 12th High.L.I. to push in his 4th Company which had not yet become involved. He then reported the conditions described above and said one Company would not suffice and asked leave to use the two Companies of 10/11th High.L.I. in his area.

-2-

10. As I did not think it would be feasible to start another organized attack I referred to you and received orders to take the trench.

11. I ordered O.C. 12th High.L.I. to carry this out with his 4th Company and 2 Companies 10/11th High.L.I. He then reported that owing to great confusion due to many killed and wounded in the trenches it would be impossible to organize a satisfactory attack before dawn. On reporting to you it was eventually decided not to carry out a second attack.

12. O.C. 12th High.L.I. was then ordered to take up original front line at 2.26 a.m.

13. As regards the operation of the 112th Infantry Brigade on our Right.
After the enemy attack at 10.25 p.m. which was beaten off some men of the Warwick Regiment came across towards LANCS SAP and got mixed up with our bombers. Although we got as far as the road down LANCS SAP there was no sign of the 112th Infantry Brigade in the INTERMEDIATE LINE. The Officer in charge of operations on this flank could get little information as to what the Battalion on his Right was doing.

14. With regard to the main operation the enemy's artillery was exceptionally heavy between 12.45 a.m. and 1.45 a.m.
From 10 p.m. to 10.25 p.m. there was a severe enemy barrage on SIXTH AVENUE, WELCH ALLEY, and LANCS TRENCH with 4.2's and Whizz Bangs.

Brigade Headquarters,
3 August, 1916.

Brig. Gen.,
Commanding,
46th Inf. Bde.

From/ 2nd Lt. A. Bryan, 12th High.L.I.

To

The Adjutant, 12th High.L.I.

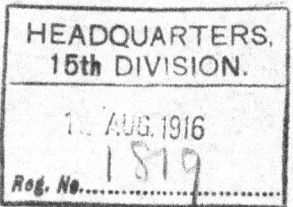

HEADQUARTERS,
15th DIVISION.

1. AUG. 1916

Reg. No. 1819

Sir,

I have the honour to submit to you the following report on the operations of the 12th High.L.I. on the night of August, 12th 1916, as far as I was connected with them. I was on the extreme left of the battalion and saw some things that may possible have escaped the notice of other officers. No 1 Platoon under my charge was in its allotted position in front of the tape by 10.10 p.m.. At this time the enemy's machine guns and rifles were firing on us heavily. At 10.15 p.m. I noticed to the left front two Germans standing waist high above an old machine gun or battery emplacement, observing us intently. I concluded that the Germans had been watching us from this point since we came into the trenches and had been studying our movements and preparations without giving us the slightest hint that he was doing so. This ws my own conclusion." I resolved that after taking the enemy"s trench I would attend to this emplacement and see it cleared out. At 10.30 p.m. I moved forward with my platoon, but had not progressed far when I was wounded in the right thigh and fell down. I ordered the men to go forward quickly, saying that I max,myself, was wounded. They did so but as far as Ix could see suffered heavily and, it being dark, I could not make out what became of them. Being along now and unable to move more than few yards, I dressed my wound and crawled into a shell hole near the emplacement where before I had seen the two Germans. I endeavoured to crawl back and give information to Headquarters but ws unable to move. I lay there observing and about 1 a.m. a German patrol of 6 men in file issued from this emplacement making straight for our line walking uprightM The moral of these men appeared to be excellent. When within say 20 yds of our wire they wheeled to the left and returned to the main trench.

The emplacement was about 120 yds in front of our trench.

(Sgd) Alfred BRYAN, 2nd Lt.
12th H.L.I.

Headquarters,
15th Division.

Forwarded for information. The photograph
shews likely places which shall receive attention

Brigade H.Q.
13 August, 1916

Brig.Gen.
Commanding, 46th I.B

SECRET.

15th Division No. 100(1)/4 G.S.

46th Inf. Bde.

44th Inf. Bde.
45th Inf. Bde.
C.R.E.
III Corps.
34th Division.
33rd D.A.
O.C., 179th Tunlg.Coy.R.E.

} For information.

Reference 15th Division Operation Order No. 74 of today:-

1. Orders have been received that the Right Division is to prepare for the attack on the 18th inst., of certain objectives on our right including the INTERMEDIATE LINE from road in S.2.d. to S.2.c.7.4.

2. To assist the above you will please push forward the sap eastwards from 70th AVENUE. By the morning of the 18th inst this sap is to be consolidated and to contain a strong point from which <u>reverse fire</u> can be brought to bear on the INTERMEDIATE LINE. To do this it will be necessary to bend the eastern portion of the sap in a North Easterly direction.

The position of this sap would be improved if it was connected to the LANCS TRENCH on the south by a connecting boyau. This the G.O.C. wishes you to endeavour to arrange.

3. You will also please establish before the 18th inst., a Barret Jack at S.2.c.7.3. so placed as to blow in the corner of the INTERMEDIATE LINE. The O.C. 179th Tunnelling Company R.E. will carry this out under your orders. He or one of his officers will report to you.

4. Machine gun and Lewis gun fire will be used continuously to prevent enemy work and reinforcement of the INTERMEDIATE LINE. You will keep in close touch with Left Brigade of Right Division.

(Sd) H. Knox

Lieut. Colonel,

15th Aug., 1916.   General Staff, 15th Division.

Copy No.____

15th. Division Operation Order No.74.

Headquarters,
15th. Division,
13th. August 1916.

Reference :-
Special Operation Map No.3.

1. The front held by the Division is shown in sketch attached.

2. Operations are to be continued by the Infantry Brigade in the Left Section to capture the SWITCH ELBOW. The 46th. Infantry Brigade will co-operate pushing forward a trench from LANCS TRENCH to join the SWITCH ELBOW.

3. Both Brigades in line will continue to harass the enemy by every means in their power. Rifles, mortars, machine and Lewis guns are to be active. Patrols to continue to push forward in front of our lines.
The 46th. Infantry Brigade will improve and lengthen all saps on their front especially the 70th. AVENUE eastern sap and those opened up by the Boring Jack.

4. The 44th. Infantry Brigade will relieve the 45th Infantry Brigade in the Left Section as arranged between Brigades. Relief to be completed by 6 p.m. on the 14th. instant.

H. Knox
Lieut. Colonel.
General Staff, 15th. Division.

Issued at   p.m.
to :-
III Corps.	copies Nos.1 & 2.	
III Corps H.A... ...	Copy No. 3.	
34th. Division.. ...	,, 4.	
4th. Australian Div..	,, 5.	
44th. Inf. Bde. ...	,, 6.	
45th. Inf. Bde. ...	,, 7.	
46th. Inf. Bde. ...	,, 8.	
9th. Gordons. ...	,, 9.	
15th. Signals. ...	,, 10.	

A.D.M.S. ...	copy No.11
A.P.M.. ...	,, 12
"A" & "Q" ...	,, 13
15th. D.A. ...	,, 14
C.R.E. ...	,, 15
23rd. D.A. ...	,, 16
War Diary. ...	,, 17
File. ...	,, 18

44th Brigade B.M.758.

H.Q., 15th Division.

With reference to 15th Division G.970 dated 12th August.-

2 Co's 8/10th Gordon Hrs.,
    PEAKE WOOD.

8/10th Gordon Hrs. (Less 2 Co's)) SCOTS
2 Co's 9th Black Watch.   ) REDOUBT.

9th Black Watch.(less 2 Co's)
    O.B. in X.26.A.

7th Cameron Hrs.)
44th M.G.Coy.   )   E.5.b.7.7.
44th T.M.Battery.)

8th Seaforth Hrs. W.29.d.8.7.
44th Bde.H.Qrs.   W.29.d.1.5.

                    Marshall
                    Brig.-Genl.,
12-8-16.   Commdg. 44th Inf.Bde.

moves will be completed by
3 p.m. 12/8/16

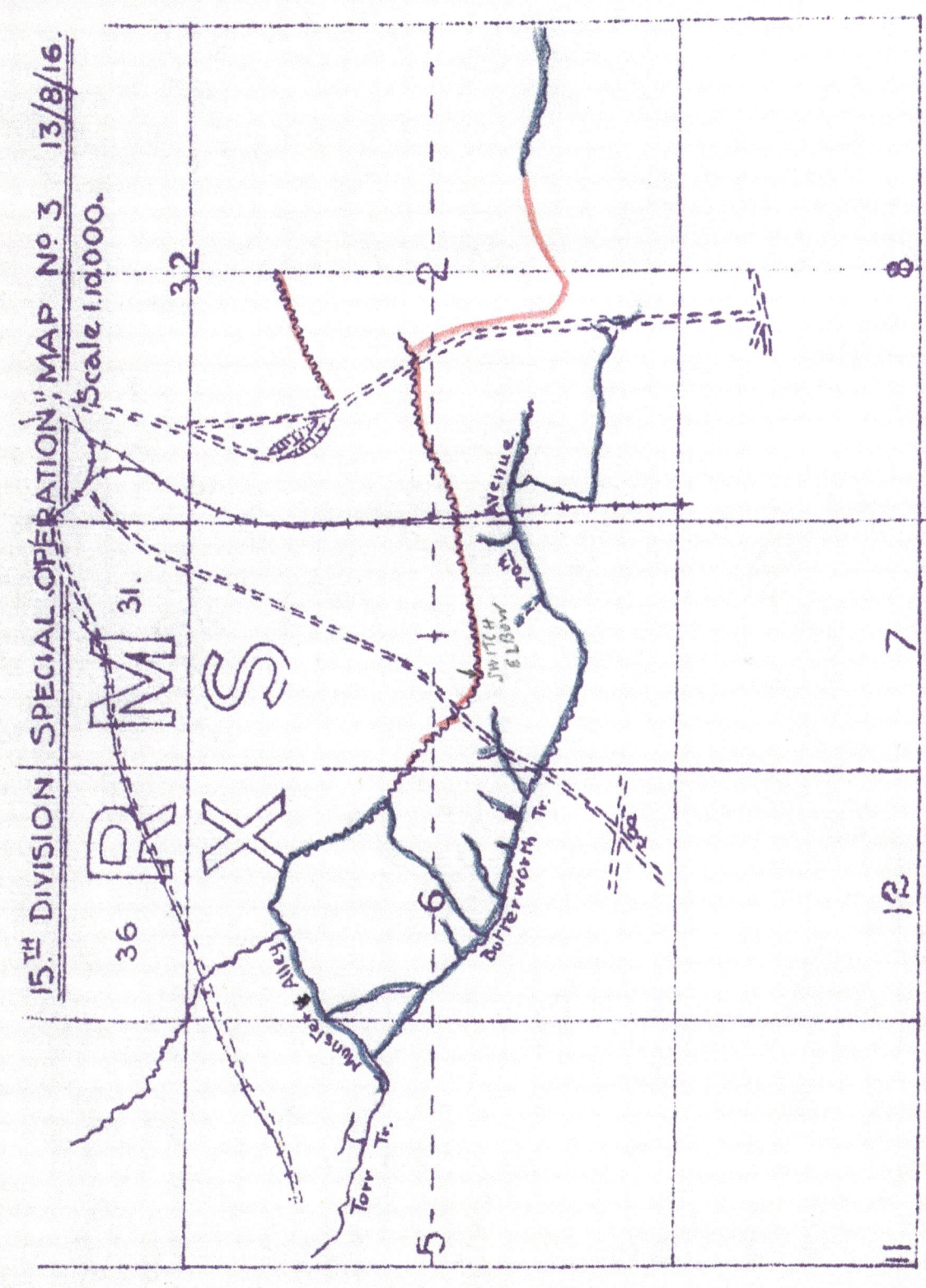

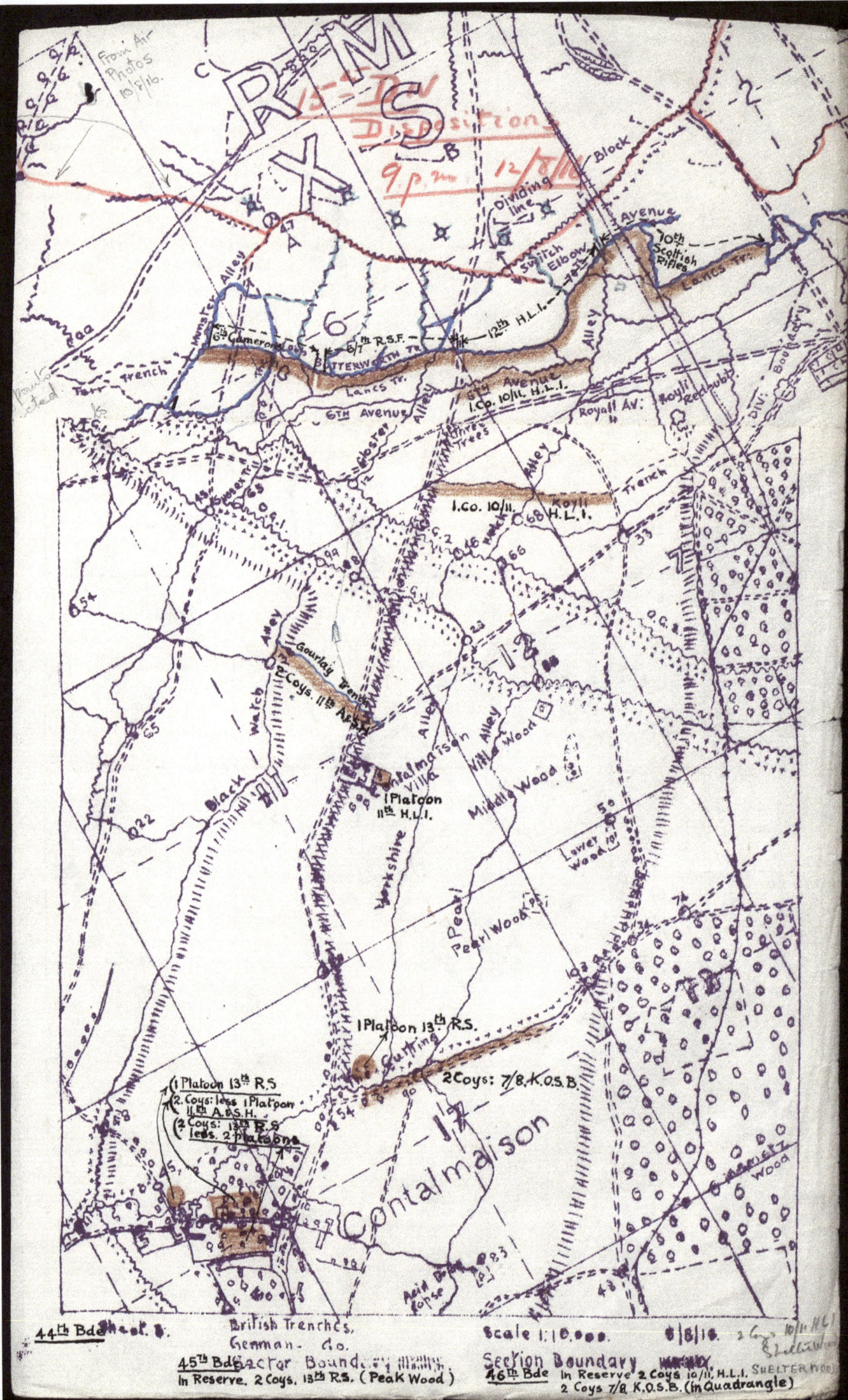

TELEPHONE RECORD.

All telephone conversations on operation subjects to be briefly noted below and initialed by officer speaking.

DATE.	HOUR.	FORMATION SPOKEN TO.	SUBJECT.
12/8/16	9.20	46th Inf Bde	Tools carried to be full sized. To be made clear to units. Genl Matheson spoke re Boring Jacks. Holes have been prepared by R.E. at wrong angles. Is doing his best to correct. Will fire at + 15". One lay has must have been near this. HK
	9.30	45th I.B.	To arrange for Lewis gun fire tonight N.E. from Munster Alley. Done. HK
12/8/16	10.2 am	45th I.B.	Bde O.O. 14 (b) G.O.C. asks if instructions have been given how far Stony Jones are to be in front of Savile. All explained to C.O.
"	10.25 am	46th I.B.	Pushes will explode at O.6. Promised there wd. be no alteration in this. Bde to ensure that ground is clear. HK
	11.10 am	3rd Corps Art	Verified that southern portion of New Boche trench N of Munster Alley is being fired on by S.O. HK
	11.22	3rd Corps Art	said only firing 50" each side of Ry. We wd. arrange direct with III Corps H.A. to bombard Southern end.

TELEPHONE RECORD.

All telephone conversations on operation subjects to be briefly noted below and initialed by officer speaking.

DATE.	HOUR.	FORMATION SPOKEN TO.	SUBJECT.
12/8/16	11.25 am	44th Bde	Orders to move 1½ Btns to replace 45th Bde Bns forward.
	11.30 am	3rd H.A.	Firing on new German tool-trench Munster Alley depends on Aeroplane wants it evacuated to be able to seize opportunities as they offer.
	11.40 am	45th Inf Bde	Would prefer owing to work not to have HA on southern portion of trench not bombarded by HA
	11.50	III Corps Art	Pointed out that 34th Div OO 44 12/8/16 does not provide for carrying our flank from S 2 a 6.2 to East from Zero onwards. GOC RA III Corps stated he had issued his orders which 34th Div wd. carry out. He will put it right.
	11.55	III Corps H.	Informed 45th Bde continue bombardment of new German Trench. Not South of 50th from Ry.
	12.40 pm	34th Div	Pointed out that III Corps Art Orders would modify their O.O. 44. as they had to barrage our right flank.
	3.5 pm	34 Div.	Say 3rd Corps HA have intimated they could not start bombardment of intermediate trench at 12 noon as all lines were cut but our trenches kept clear later on

TELEPHONE RECORD.

All telephone conversations on operation subjects to be briefly noted below and initialed by officer speaking.

DATE.	HOUR.	FORMATION SPOKEN TO.	SUBJECT.
CR.	3.20 p.m	3ʳᵈ Corps	consequence. Will let us know later when bom'bat will begin & end. 46ᵗʰ Bde informed. BGGS 3ʳᵈ Corps enquired if we were satisfied that Anzac arrangements for covering our left tonight included M.G. fire. Replied yes, + confirmed by phoning 4ᵗʰ Aust Div.
	4.15 p.m	IIIʳᵈ Corps H.A.	Enquired for 46ᵗʰ I.B. time of finish of bombardment. Informed not yet known. HA IIIʳᵈ Corps will inform directly completed. Probably only just beginning now. Informed 46ᵗʰ Brigade
	5.2 p.m	IIIʳᵈ Corps HA	Report shooting about to begin & not expected to finish before 7.30 p.m
	5.10 p.m	34 Div G	Information from him as above CR
	11.53 p.m	From 45 Bde. (III Corps informed)	Message from Right Battalion 11.40 p.m SWITCH occupied by three Companies.
13.8.16	12.2 A.M	From 23ʳᵈ D.A. (verbally) (III Corps informed)	Liaison Officer R.A. reports 3 Coys Camerons in the SWITCH and digging hard - Stated to have been very difficult to find SWITCH LINE. Some Anzacs have come up & joined them

TELEPHONE RECORD.

All telephone conversations on operation subjects to be briefly noted below and initialed by officer speaking.

DATE.	HOUR.	FORMATION SPOKEN TO.	SUBJECT.
13.8.16	12.5 A₂	23 D.A. (verbally)	Attack on Right by 45 Bde at first held up by M.G. fire - Second attempt successful
"	12.6 A₂	Bde 45 Bde.	6/7 R.S.F. first held up by M.G. fire - 6th Cameron digging in on SWITCH LINE.
"	12.35 A₂	23 D.A. (verbally)	3 Coys Right Batt 45 Bde got in after a good fight - Three Coys left Batt. are in and digging & putting stops on right. 46 Bde are in "No Man's Land" going to shove up more Coys & push home attack. Heavy barrage on O.G.1 & O.G.2
"	12.35 A₂	General Matheson	3 Coys 12 H.L.I. are still out - He has ordered a fourth to push in. He wants to know if he is to use another Battalion to attack if that does not succeed.
"	12.45 A₂	G.I.O.I	Spoke to Bde 46 Bde - GOC wishes you to take the trench & bring up another Battalion - He does not wish you to shove another Batt. in if

(contd)

TELEPHONE RECORD.

All telephone conversations on operation subjects to be briefly noted below and initialed by officer speaking.

DATE.	HOUR.	FORMATION SPOKEN TO.	SUBJECT.
		(Cont'd)	There is no prospect of taking it. B.G.b. said then that case he would have to go up & conduct operations from Batt: H.Q. B.G.b. said he would not leave Bde H.Q. until G.S.O.I had spoken S.O.C. He would get Batt: ready to move up.
13.8.16	1 A.m	D.m. 23 DA	Centre and Right Companies of 6 Camerons are digging to a depth of 2½ feet — Have no shell fire all their casualties caused by bullets at a range of 500 to 600 yds. 3 Coys 6/7 R.S.F believe to have entered trench but not yet certain. P.T.O

TELEPHONE RECORD.

All telephone conversations on operation subjects to be briefly noted below and initialed by officer speaking.

DATE.	HOUR.	FORMATION SPOKEN TO.	SUBJECT.
13/8/16	12.55 AM	G.O.C.	Spoke Genl Matheson who said attacking troops had lost their Officers & situation is confused. In reply to question by G.O.C., B.G.C. said 45. Bde could not help. Asked by G.O.C. if B.G.C. would send up a Staff Officer, he said he already had one up. B.G.C. said he was going to put in two Coys 10/11 H.L.I. with a Coy 12 H.L.I.
	1.5 AM	Capt Ryan	G.S.O. I asked Capt Ryan if B.G.C. 46 Bde can give any information as to what he would like Artillery to do & pointed out that barrage can be brought on to the trench E. of the Railway and brought closer in W. of the Railway. Capt Ryan said B.G.C. was working an order & would speak in a moment.

TELEPHONE RECORD.

All telephone conversations on operation subjects to be briefly noted below and initialed by officer speaking.

DATE.	HOUR.	FORMATION SPOKEN TO.	SUBJECT.
13/8/16	1.20p	III Corps	G.S.O I said left Brigade had got in and were digging. Situation in Right Brigade was not clear; nobody but a few wounded had returned & there was a good deal of firing. No confirmation of the rumour that there had been a German attack on Right Battn. Right Bde.
	1.30p	45 Bde	Bn. gave following message received from 13th R.S. Fr:- "OC Centre Coy timed 11.25 pm stating SWITCH occupied. Heavy hostile rifle fire. Heavy machine gun fire from right - also asks for reinforcements for right." 4th Coy sent up on Platoon. Bn. says 46 Bde are not in & G.S.O I told him that G.O.C. had ordered another 3 Companies in to attack. Bn. says report from

TELEPHONE RECORD.

All telephone conversations on operation subjects to be briefly noted below and initialed by officer speaking.

DATE.	HOUR.	FORMATION SPOKEN TO.	SUBJECT.
			6 Cameron are favourable - They are digging in. Bn Says that Anzacs are digging up MONSTER ALLEY. - also that rifle fire from right was troublesome. Informed Bn. that S.O.C. had told 46 Bde to push on. Bn. said 6/7 R.S.F were in alright
13/8/16	1.32 AM	S.O.C	Spoke B.G.C 46 Bde & said 45 Bde reported that 6/7 R.S.F. are feeling M.G. fire & Rifle fire from the right which can be relieved by 46 Bde attack. Questioned as to R.A. assistance B.G.C said that Barrage cannot be any nearer as it would interfere with the putting out of Strong posts - B.G.C. could not say as to the system of Runners. B.G.C. reported that M.G.s. were doing all they can - Gordons still digging according to last report

TELEPHONE RECORD.

All telephone conversations on operation subjects to be briefly noted below and initialed by officer speaking.

DATE.	HOUR.	FORMATION SPOKEN TO.	SUBJECT.
13/8/18	1.45 A	34 Div	Received - Section Rifle say they were not quite up to road but nearly so - Some of Warwicks (34 Di) were mixed up with them.
			G.S.O. I pointed out that we were digging in "beyond enemy front line" & that some Warwicks were mixed up and asked 34th Div. for any information - 34 Di wires all cut & could give no information.
	1.58 A	B.G.C. 46 Bde	Report message received from O.C. 12 K.L.R. "Have sent for Coy Comdrs to organize attack but owing to confusion existing in trenches from the disorganized companies, wounded & intensity of MG fire & R.A. barrage on our front I consider successful attack beyond hope - Consider it requires fresh Batt. & fresh preparations" - B.G.C. agrees with this B.G.C. informed that G.O.C. does not want

TELEPHONE RECORD.

All telephone conversations on operation subjects to be briefly noted below and initialed by officer speaking.

DATE.	HOUR.	FORMATION SPOKEN TO.	SUBJECT.
			to waste men on a futile attack. Told to find out situation in No man's land & in meantime carry on preparations for attack but not to carry it out till GOC orders.
13/8/16	2.7 AM	45 Bde	Reports MG fire coming from direction of S.2.a.3.½ & further E of the Elbow. G.S.O.I said he would get more guns on. 45 Bde reported 1 Coy 11 A&SH moved up from GOURLAY Trench to front line and 1 Coy 11 A&SH from CONTALMAISON to GOURLAY TR. - B.G.C. think R.S.F. can hold on & have been ordered to do so at all costs. G.S.O.I explained situation with 46 Bde & asked if SWITCH could be bombarded almost up to elbow - 45 Bd think quite safe to bombard 100ˣ from point of elbow. B.G.C. told to consolidate all positions & thin out before daylight. Reported strong point is progressing. G.O.C. congratulated B.G.C.

TELEPHONE RECORD.

All telephone conversations on operation subjects to be briefly noted below and initialed by officer speaking.

DATE.	HOUR.	FORMATION SPOKEN TO.	SUBJECT.
13/8/18	2.20 am	46 Bde.	G.S.O. I told B.G.C. that 45 Bde will hold on. Informed that G.O.C. required report as soon as all 46 Bde are back so that R.A. action can be taken. Further message from O.C. 12 H.L.I. repeats opinion that successful attack hopeless
	2.27 am	—	G.S.O. I arranged with R.A. to turn fire on to suspected M.G. at S.2.A.
	3.6 am	46 Bde	B.G.C. reported "no man's land" clear except for wounded — told to report when all clear. B.G.C. was informed that R.A. had been turned on to suspected M.G's & that barrage has been shortened. G.S.O. I pointed out necessity for doing something to assist 45 Bde & that O.C. 12 H.L.I. must do all he can in this matter with T.M's & M.G's

TELEPHONE RECORD.

All telephone conversations on operation subjects to be briefly noted below and initialed by officer speaking.

DATE.	HOUR.	FORMATION SPOKEN TO.	SUBJECT.
13.8.16	3.56 AM	—	G.S.O. I arranged with RA to bring back barrage on to SWITCH LINE E. of portion captured.
	4 AM.	45 Bde	Informed as above.

"A" Form.
MESSAGES AND SIGNALS.

TO	44th Inf Bde	53 D A
	45 Inf Bde	
	46th Inf Bde	

Sender's Number: 2.Q15　　Day of Month: 12th　　　　AAA

Following extracts from aeroplane reconnaissance this morning AAA SWITCH LINE destroyed except from X.6.a.7.4. to X.6.a.6.2 and from S.1.b.1½ to S.2.a.4.1. AAA Shooting on ELBOW in S.1.d. 11 to 11.30 most effective with many direct hits AAA No report on condition of NEW TRENCH from X.6.a.2.9. to 3.5

From: 15th Div
Time: 2/1

Capt 65

15th Divⁿ

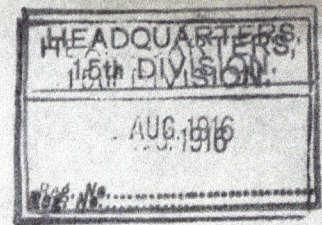

Air Reconnaissance 10.30 a.m. - 11.45 a.m. 12/8/16.
of the area POZIERES - MARTINPUICH - HIGH WOOD.

1. The switch line is destroyed from X.6.a.5.7. to X.6.a.7.4.
   " " " " " " X.6.a.8.2. to S.1.a.1.½.
   " " " " " continuously from S.2.a.4.1. to
   HIGH WOOD.

2. The portions of the switch line which are still good are from -

   (a) X.6.a.7.4. to X.6.a.8.2.
   (b) S.1.a.1.½. to S.2.a.4.1.

3. The communication trench from the Switch Line to the Intermediate
   Line is destroyed except for the portion between S.2.c.5.7½.
   and 8.6½.
       The Corner of the Intermediate has suffered but is not
   obliterated.
       The remainder of the Intermediate Line is intact.

4. The shooting between 11 a.m. - 11.30 a.m. on the Switch Elbow
   & Switch Line in S.1.d. was most effective the shells falling
   right into the trench consistently.

5. Our infantry could be seen in MUNSTER ALLEY up as far as
   X.5.b.9.3½.
       Germans could be seen in the same trench just South of the
   junction with their new trench at X.6.a.1½.5.
       The portion between X.5.b.9.3½. and X.6.a.1½.5. did not
   appear to be occupied.

6. The communication trench from the Switch Line in M.23.d. to the
   road cutting at M.23.d.4.8. has been destroyed.
       The continuation of this communication trench which goes to
   the road at X.27.d.6.8. now carries straight on back parallel
   & close to the road to the 3rd line at EAUCOURT L'ABBAYE at
   M.23.c.½.6.

7. The trench running from M.32.a.6.7. to M.23.a.3.6. is continued
   into the road cutting at M.28.d.9.1.

8. The trench S. of MARTINPUICH reported by the 3rd Sqd. R.F.C.
   running from S.2.a.5.8. to S.2.b.3.9. does not appear to be
   completed.

9. The German trench from the N.W. corner of HIGH WOOD which runs
   through S.3.d. & c. appeared to be occupied. It has not been
   continued any further west.

"I"
12th August, 1916.

                                            Captain,
                                       General Staff, III Corps.

<u>URGENT.</u>　　　　　　　　　　　　　　　　<u>SECRET.</u>

　　　　　　　　　　　　　　　　　　　　<u>15th Division.</u>
　　　　　　　　　　　　　　　　　　　　<u>No.100/4 G.a.</u>
<u>46th Inf. Bde.</u>

1.　The G.O.C. wishes you to push forward all preparations with a view to continuing the attack which you commenced last night.　He wishes you to be prepared to attack at once should he order you to do so.　It is particularly important that work be carried on on the trenches opened up by the pusher, the artillery covering fire will be arranged to admit of this work being done.

2.　Acknowledge.

　　　　　　　　　　　　　　　　　　　　　[signature]
　　　　　　　　　　　　　　　　　　　　Lieut Colonel,
<u>13th August, 1916.</u>　　<u>General Staff, 15th Division.</u>

G982

"A"

Estimated Casualties
12th H.L.I. :-

3 Officers Killed
11　"　Wounded
200 other Ranks Killed + wounded

[signature]
Lt Col.

2.50 An
13/8/16

SECRET.   COPY NO. 3

34TH DIVISIONAL ARTILLERY OPERATION ORDER NO.45.

Ref. 1/5,000 Map.   12.8.1916.

1.   The 4th Australian Division is attacking on the night of the 12/13th August the following Line:-
        R.34.a.8.6. - 65 - 05 - R.33.b.5.5. - 32.
     The 15th Division will attack the SWITCH LINE from about S.1.d.9.9. to the junction of MUNSTER ALLEY on the night of the 12/13th.
     The 34th Division will continue their attack to complete the capture of the Intermediate Line.

2.   The 34th Divisional Artillery will barrage from BAPAUME ROAD, inclusive, to 50 yards south of Tramline, being careful to search the Tramline as far west as can be done with safety.
     152nd Brigade R.F.A. (2 18-pdr Batteries) and 160th Brigade R.F.A. will barrage new Trench about X.35.d.4.6. - X.6.a.1.9. thence to X.6.a.2.9.
     ~~160th Brigade R.F.A. will also Barrage Tramline as far as.~~
     Dividing point for Brigades R.35.d.8.3.
     152nd Brigade R.F.A. will overlap BAPAUME ROAD.
     160th Brigade Howitzer Battery will have one Gun on Machine Gun emplacement 20 yards S of R.35.d.3.5. Remaining Guns on Tramline and Track in R.36.c. and M.31.d.
    Times and Rates of fire:-
    0.0. to 0.5.   4 Rounds per Gun per Minute.
    0.5. to 0.10.   2 Rounds per Gun per minute.
    0.10.to 1 hour.   1 Round per Gun per minutes.
    1 hour onwards, ordinary night firing on these Lines.

3.   Zero hour will be 10-30 p.m.

4.   Watches will be synchronised by an Officer who will call at Brigade Headquarters between 5-30 p.m. and 6 p.m. to-night.

5.   Acknowledge.

                                            Armas

Issued at 2-15 p.m.   Major.
   Copy No.1. 3rd Corps R.A.   Brigade Major R.A.
        2. 4th Aust.Divn.   34th Division.
        3. 15th Division.
        4. 34th Division.
        5. Lahore Division.
        6. 23rd Divl.Artillery.
        7. 152nd F.A.Brigade.
        8. 160th   -do-
     9 - 11 Diary.

S E C R E T.
15th Division No. 100/4 G.a.

44th Inf. Bde.
45th Inf. Bde.
46th Inf. Bde.
34th Div.
4th Australian Div.

Reference 15th Div. O.O. 73 para. 4 (iv).

Following is a summary of the action being taken by artillery other than Left Group Divisional Artillery in tonight's attack :-

(a). At O.1 H.A. III Corps all available Hows. a salvos about 500 yards north of the front we are attacking.
They will then fire till + 1 hour on road and railway in R.36.c. and various objectives in rear.

(b). O.O. to O.4 all 60-pdr. and 4.7" batteries will fire shrapnel on an area South East to South West of MARTINPUICH.

(c). O.O to 1 hour one 60-pdr or 4.7" battery will fire shrapnel on sunken road in R.36.c.

(d). 34th Div. Art. will barrage BAPAUME ROAD inclusive to 50 yards South of Railway searching the Railway as far west as safety will allow.

(e). 1st Divl. Arty. Group in addition to supporting their own attack will search and sweep the country 300 yards behind and including the SWITCH LINE from the MARTINPUICH - BAZENTIN LE PETIT ROAD inclusive to road in M.33.c.

(f). All counter batteries will be active.

12th Aug., 1916.

Lieut. Colonel,
General Staff, 15th Division.

ARTILLERY INSTRUCTIONS NO.56
BY
THE G.O.C., R.A., IIIrd Corps.

HEADQUARTERS.
15th DIVISION.
12 AUG. 1916
Copy No. 1

Headquarters, R.A.,
IIIrd Corps.
12th August, 1916

1. The 4th Australian Division is attacking on the night 12/13th August the following line :-

R.34.a.8.6 - 65 - 05 - R.33.b.5.5 - 32.

The 15th Division will attack the SWITCH LINE from about S.1.d.9.9 to the junction of MUNSTER ALLEY on the night of the 12/13th.

The 34th Division will continue their attack to complete the capture of the Intermediate line.

2. <u>Heavy Artillery, IIIrd Corps.</u>

(a) at 0.1 will fire a salvo of all available Hows. on the line M.31.d.3.0 - S.1.b.6.6 - S.2.a.3.6.

(b) Will then fire till +1 hour at a moderate rate with selected batteries at sunken road from R.36.c.6.1 to M.31.d.5.3.

Trench S.1.b.6.8 to M.32.c.1.4.

MARTINPUICH.

(c) 0.0 to 0.4 all 60-pdr and 4.7-inch batteries to fire shrapnel on area M.32.d.25.32 - M.32.d.10.85 - M.32.c.3.5 - M.31.d.6.9 - M.31.d.0.5 - S.2.a.0.7.

(d) 0.0 to 1 hour. One 60-pdr or 4.7-inch battery to fire shrapnel at sunken road by railway.

(e) Counter battery work to be active from + 0.4 to 1 hour but to be intense from + 0.4 to + 0.15.

3. The <u>34th Divl. Artillery</u> will barrage from BAPAUME ROAD, inclusive, to 50 yards south of railway, being careful to search the railway as far west as can be done with safety.

0.0 to 0.5 Intense rate of fire.

0.5 to 0.10 Moderate rate of fire.

0.10 to 1 hour steady.

1 hour onwards, ordinary night firing on these lines.

4. The <u>23rd Divl. Artillery Group.</u> will act in accordance with orders issued by 15th Division.

- 2 -

5. The <u>1st Divl. Artillery Group</u> will, as far as possible, consistent with the needs of the 34th Division, search and sweep the country 300 yards behind and including the SWITCH LINE from road, inclusive, through S.2.a. to road in M.33.c. and also the West edge of HIGH WOOD.

6. XVth and XIIIth Corps have been asked to counter all hostile batteries in their zone that fire on IIIrd Corps front.

Intense from 0.0 to 0.15, and then as required.

7. Zero time will be 10.30 p.m.

8. Watches will be synchronized at 46th Infantry Bde. Headquarters, SHELTER WOOD at 5.15 p.m to-day, 12th instant.

Representatives of Artillery Groups to be present.

9. ACKNOWLEDGE.

Issued at   am

L W Lewer
Major,
Staff Officer to G.O.C.,R.A.,
IIIrd Corps.

Copy. No.	
1	15th Division
2	34th Division
3	1st Divl. Arty.
4	15th Div. Arty.
5	23rd Div. Arty.
6	34th Div. Arty.
7	Heavy Artillery.
8	No.34th Squadron, R.F.C.
9	No.6 Kite Balloon Section
10	No.14 Kite Balloon Section.
11	Arty. 15th Corps.
12	Arty. 13th Corps.
13	Arty. 1st Anzac Corps
14	Arty. 4th Army.
15	IIIrd Corps "G.S".
16-19	Filed.

HEADQUARTERS,
15th DIVISION.
12 AUG. 1916
Reg. No. 1791

SECRET.

COPY NO. 6

ADDENDUM NO. 2

to

III CORPS OPERATION ORDER NO. 108.

12.8.16.

1. The 34th DIVISION will also attack the rest of the INTERMEDIATE LINE still in possession of the enemy, at the same time as the 15th DIVISION attack the SWITCH LINE, i.e. 10.30 p.m. to-night.

2. The Contact Patrol Aeroplane will fly over the 34th Division also, when flares will be shewn.

3. Correct time will be distributed by a Staff Officer of III Corps at the Brigade H.Q. at SHELTER WOOD, as follows :-

   (i) Representatives of 112th Bde. & 1st & 15th Div.Arty.Groups
                                                        4.45 p.m.

   (ii) " " " " " 15th Div.Brigades & supporting Artillery
                                                   Groups ... 5.0. p.m.

   (iii) " " " " " III Corps Heavy Artillery
                                                       5.15 p.m.

4. Acknowledge by wire.

for B.d.S.attye Major
Brigadier-General,
General Staff
III CORPS.

Issued by S.D.R. at 11.45 am.

To all recipients of O.O.No.108.

Copy No 17

Supplementary Orders to Infantry Brigade Order No 84

Reference
15th Div. Special
Operation Map
No 1. dated
10/8/16.

Brigade H.Q.
12/8/16

HEADQUARTERS.
15th DIVISION.
12 AUG. 1916
Reg. No. 1792

1. Reference para 8 (a) of Order No 84
The communication trenches will not be blown until zero and the officers in charge belonging to 179th Tunnelling Coy. R.E. will be responsible for carrying this out.
At this hour there should be nobody between the captured trench and our present front line.
Para 8 (b) is therefore cancelled.

2. O.C., 10th Sco.Rif. will man that portion of 70th AVENUE East of the railway and keep up rapid fire on the enemy's SWITCH TRENCH East of the railway, care being taken not to direct the fire west of the Railway.

3. The 112th Inf. Bde. on our right will at zero attack INTERMEDIATE TRENCH from S.2.d.3½.5. to S.2.c.8.5. Their action will be to capture that trench and establish a bombing post 60 yds north of S.2.c.8.5.
To assist this operation O.C., 10th Sco.Rif. will have two bombing squads in the sap running N.E. from LANCS TRENCH ready to co-operate with the Royal Warwickshire Regt. which will be making the attack.
O.C., 10th Sco.Rif. will get into touch with O.C. that battalion on receipt of these orders.
The 112th Infantry Brigade propose to dig along the EAST side of the road, marking the right boundary of our area, to connect with the German INTERMEDIATE LINE at S.2.c.8.5. at the same time O.C., 10th Sco. Rif. will arrange to open up the Sap running N.E. from LANCS TRENCH to the East side of the road so as to cut into the trench being dug by the 112th Infantry Brigade.

4. With reference to paras 10 and 11 of Order No 84 trench mortars and Machine guns will be careful not to fire on the INTERMEDIATE TRENCH South of S.2.c.8.8. but one Stokes Mortar will be told off to open fire at S.2.c.8.5. at zero and quickly traverse northwards along the trench as far as S.2.c.8.8., but not to return south of that point after reaching it.

5. With reference to Order No 84, Para 14 last line on page 4 it must be clearly understood that picks and shovels are to be carried, not merely entrenching tools.

6. During the operation all units in the Brigade will be dressed ready to move at a moments notice. O.C. 7/8th K.O.Sco.Bord. and 10/11th High.L.I. will each detail an officer to report at Brigade Headquarters at 10.15 p.m. for the purpose of taking any orders necessary.

7. O.C., 7/8th K.O.Sco.Bord. will detail a party of one officer and 25 men to report to Lieut. ALSTON, 10/11th High.L.I. at MIDDLE WOOD at 9.30 p.m. for the purpose of carrying forward bombs etc, to Left Battalion Dump vide para 15 (a) of 46th Brigade Order No 84.

                                              Captain,
                                              Bde Maj.,
                                              46th Inf.Bde.

Issued at 11.45 a
    through Signals.

Copy No		
1	File
2	War Diary
3	7/8th K.O.Sco.Bord.
4	10th Sco.Rif.
5	10/11th High.L.I.
6	12th High.L.I.
7	46th M.G. Company
8	46th T.M.Battery
9	Staff Captain
10	Brigade Signal Officer
11	73rd Field Coy.R.E.
12	O.C.,"G" Coy,9th Gordons
13	Medium T.M.Battery
14	179th Tunnelling Coy.R.E.
15	45th Inf.Bde.
16	112th Inf.Bde.
17	15th Division.
18	Spare
19	Spare.

War Diary
7/8th K.O.S.B. [?]
10th A.Co. R.F.
10th [?] Argyle L.I.
12th Argyle L.I.
45th M.G. Coy.
46th T.M. Battery
Staff Captain
Brigade Signalling Officer
73rd Field Coy. R.E.
O.C. G Coy 9th Gordons
Medium T.M. Battery.
179th Tunnelling Coy. R.E.
44th Inf. Bde.
45th Inf. Bde.
112th Inf. Bde.
15th Division. ✓

Reference 46th Inf. Bde. order
No. 84 paragraph 2,
  Zero-time will be – 10.30 P.M.
  Arkenburgh [?].

SECRET

HEADQUARTERS
15th DIVISION.
12 AUG. 1916
Reg. No. 1795

[signature]
Brigade H.Q.,
12 Aug. 1916.

D. Chapman
Capt.
for Brigade Major
46th Inf. Bde.

SECRET   Copy No...

46th Infantry Brigade Order No 84.

Reference Special
Operation Map No 1   Headquarters,
dated 10/8/16   46th Inf.Bde.
attached herewith.   11/8/16.

1. 4th Australian Division on night 12/13th
August is attacking on the line R.34.a.8.6. - 6.5. -
0.3 - R.33.b.5.5. - 3.2.

2. On the night August 12/13th the 15th Division will
attack the enemy SWITCH LINE from S.1.d.9.9. to Point 47
in X.6.a. (MUNSTER ALLEY).
    The 4th Australian Division have been asked to
assist by forming a defensive flank on the left of
the attack.
    Zero time will be communicated later. (10.30 p.m.)

3. The 46th Infantry Brigade will attack on the
right, the 45th Infantry Brigade will attack on the
left. Dividing line between Brigades 30 yards E. of
junction of GLOSTER ALLEY with SWITCH LINE (SWITCH ELBOW).

4. (i)   The barrage established at 2 p.m., 10th
August on the German SWITCH LINE will be maintained.
    On the 11th and 12th instants the Heavy
Artillery will bombard certain points in the
SWITCH LINE. Between the hours of 10 a.m. and
1 p.m. on those days, 70th AVENUE, parts of
LANCS TRENCH, GLOSTER ALLEY SAP and MUNSTER ALLEY
SAP will be evacuated.

    (ii) Up to fifteen minutes before zero on the
12/13th activity on the front of attack will be
normal. At fifteen minutes before zero the
normal barrage will be brought on to the trenches
to be attacked.

    (iii) On night of 12/13th an intense bombardment
of the objective by the Left Group Divisional
Artillery III Corps will commence at zero hours.
The fire will lift at the following times:--
        0.2   ...   lift 100 yards
        0.3   ...   lift 50 yards
        0.5   ...   lift 50 yards
        0.7   ...   lift 50 yards.

    (iv) Detailed instructions regarding the action
of the Left Group Divisional Artillery III Corps
and Heavy and Corps Artillery will be issued.

5. (a) The 12th High.L.I. will attack that portion
of the GERMAN SWITCH LINE allotted to 46th Inf.Bde.

    (b) The frontage is approximately 300 yards, and
at the centre of the frontage the objective is about
150 yards from our front line.
This distance increases to about 230 yards opposite
the left flank of the attack and decreases to about
140 yards on the right flank of the attack.
O.C., 12th High.L.I. will therefore take special steps
to see that the attack starts on a frontage parallel
to the position, and for this purpose the line is to be
marked out by him with tape beforehand, and at a
distance of from about 140 yards to 150 yards from the
enemy's trench.
O.C., 73rd Field Coy. R.E. will provide the tape.

(c) The attack is to be made with three companies, each with two platoons in the first wave and two platoons in the second wave; the third wave will consist of the fourth company in line ; but this wave should not be launched in the attack unless required. Care must be taken not to overcrowd the objective when taken.

(d) The attacking troops are to be in position ready to attack at zero, at which hour it will move forward to the attack close under the artillery barrage which lifts at 0.2

(e) Lewis guns will accompany the first two waves.

(f) A special bombing party will be told off to move with the first or second wave to bomb eastward towards the railway and to hold the trench whilst the stops mentioned in sub-para (g) below are being constructed. These bombers should be supported by a Lewis Gun. When the stops are completed this bombing party will fall back on the back stop.
The garrison at this point must have a Lewis gun to support it.

(g) Special parties will be told off to erect stops in the captured trench as follows :--

    (i) A forward stop immediately opposite the *right* flank of the attack about 80 yards west of the railway.

    (ii) A back stop at a point 40 yards west of the forward stop. Each of these parties will consist of 1 N.C.O. and 3 men to be detailed by O.C., 73rd Field Coy. R.E. and an officer and 7 men to be detailed by 12th Bn High.L.I.

O.C., 12th High.L.I. will be responsible for the construction of these stops. Each infantryman of these two parties will carry 20 sandbags. In addition the infantry parties will carry 4 picks and 8 shovels. These parties will follow close after the second wave but will not form part of the second wave.
O.C., 12th High.L.I. will issue instructions where these parties are to assemble.

(h) A party will be told off to form a stop on the left of the objective until touch is obtained with the 45th Inf. Bde., but no bombing is to take place into the enemy trench west of this point.

6. As soon as the SWITCH TRENCH is captured infantry patrols are to be pushed out inside our barrage for a distance of 150 to 200 yards under cover of which two strong posts are to be constructed. 100 yds in advance of SWITCH LINE, one being sited opposite each of the two new communication trenches.
Shell holes should be selected to form the foundation of these strong points . They will take the shape of a Cross as described in Brigade Memo. No 10 forwarded to units on the 4th August.
The garrison will consist of one officer and one platoon with 2 Lewis Guns for each post. A Vickers gun will eventually form part of the garrison of each post and these will be established as soon as the posts are complete, under arrangements to be made by O.C., 46th M.G. Company with O.C., 12th High.L.I.

The wiring of these strong posts will be carried out as follows :-

(i) Dumps of wire pickets and mauls, etc, will be assembled beforehand at places selected by O.C., 12th High.L.I.

(ii) The two parties told off by O.C., 12th High.L.I. to erect wire at the strong posts will take the first consignment of wire, etc, across and begin work.

(iii) Each of these two parties will be accompanied by 1 N.C.O. and 10 men of 73rd Field Coy.R.E.. O.C., 12th High.L.I. will arrange with O.C., 73rd Field Company. R.E. where and at what time these parties will assemble.

(iv) O.C., 10/11th High.L.I. will place at the disposal of O.C. 12th High.L.I. 2 parties each consisting of one officer and 25 men to carry over the remaining material required for wiring. O.C., 12th High.L.I. to arrange with O.C. 10/11th High.L.I. hour and place these parties are to report. These parties are to be taken from the two companies referred to in para № 12

7. The remaining portions of the attacking force not employed on other duties will be employed in at once turning portions of the captured trench into a fire trench to be connected later.

If this is considered inadvisable by the senior officer on the spot after the trench is captured these portions of the attacking force will be employed in digging in, in front of the captured line.

8. Communication Trenches to Objective

(a) The communication trenches Y.K.L. and W.V. shown on plan issued with preliminary order will be undermined with Pipe pusher machine and these will be exploded at zero.
This will be carried out by O.C., 179 Tunnelling Company.

(b) In lining out, preliminary to the advance, care must be taken to allow for the effect of the explosion.

(c) As soon as the objective is captured the construction of the two communication trenches will be carried out by half a company of 9th Gordon Highlanders (Pioneers) 1 Platoon on each trench.
These platoons will assemble at zero less 45 minutes as follows :-
That for the left Communication trench, in LANCASHIRE TRENCH just east of WELCH ALLEY. This portion of the trench being handed over by 10th Sco.Rif. for this purpose.

(d) O.C., 12th High.L.I. will decide at what time these parties are to commence their work.

That for the right communication trench Y.K.L. in 70th AVENUE, East of Point D.

4.

9. Communication trenches to Strong Points

O.C., 12th High.L.I. will arrange to connect the strong points with the German SWITCH LINE as soon as possible.

10. Trench Mortars

(a) O.C. Medium Trench Mortar Battery and O.C. 46th Trench Mortar Battery will arrange to bring fire to bear on the German SWITCH LINE from where the Railway crosses it to the east and also on the INTERMEDIATE LINE.

(b) Fire will be opened at zero and will be intense for 10 minutes and intermittent for the rest of the night whilst our working parties are consolidating the position

(c) O.C., 10th Sco.Rif. will be prepared to provide a party of one Officer and 25 men to carry Stokes Ammunition from MIDDLE WOOD to mortar position if called on by O.C., 46th Trench Mortar Battery in which case 46th Trench Mortar Battery will provide guides to meet this party at MIDDLE WOOD Dump.

11. Machine Guns.

O.C., 46th Machine Gun Company will support the attack by firing on the German SWITCH LINE to the East of the Railway and on the INTERMEDIATE TRENCH.

12. Support

O.C., 10/11th High.L.I. will detail two companies to occupy the front system of the left sub-section as follows:—

One company to 6th AVENUE
One company to KOYLI TRENCH.

The above to be in position at zero minus 60 minutes moving via PEARL ALLEY and WELCH ALLEY. These two companies will then come under orders of O.C., 12th High.L.I. to whom they will report arrival.

The carrying parties mentioned in para 6 (iv) will be drawn from these companies.

13. Contact Aeroplane Patrol

A contact aeroplane patrol will fly over the objective at 6 a.m., 13th inst. It will sound a klaxton horn and the advanced line of infantry will then display red flares at the bottom of the trenches. The use of these flares and their reason is to be explained to all ranks beforehand.

14. Dress

Fighting order. Care to be taken to see that water bottles are full and iron rations complete.

220 rounds S.A.A. to be carried. Bombing squads will carry not less than 50 rounds S.A.A. per man in addition to 12 bombs.

All other ranks will carry two bombs.

At least 50% of leading waves will carry tools.

5.

A proportion of men will be told off to carry Very lights, and rifle grenades.

Mills cups with pusher rod should be taken as they will be useful in dislodging enemy from shell holes

A proportion of men will be told off to carry red flares for signalling to contact aeroplanes.

Every man will carry two sandbags.

15. **Dumps.**
(a) The battalion dump for Bombs will consist of 3,000 bombs (250 boxes) and will be situated in the trench running from WELCH ALLEY to SCOTCH ALLEY and which lies between LANCS TRENCH and 6th AVENUE.

O.C., 12th High.L.I. will arrange for an advance battalion dump from which to supply captured trench and strong points.

Brigade Headquarters will keep the Battalion dump full. O.C. 12th High.L.I. will be responsible for keeping Battalion Advanced Dump full and he can use portions of the supporting companies of the 10/11th High.L.I. for this purpose.

O.C., 12th High.L.I. will be responsible for ~~running~~ pushing forward bombs from advanced battalion depot with other parties of his own battalion.

(b) The following will be dumped in the vicinity of the left hand communication trench about point W.

(i) 50 boxes S.A.A.
(ii) Wiring material for strong points and for captured line.
(iii) 32 Petrol tins filled with water and 70 Iron rations for strong points.
(iv) 500 Very lights (5 boxes)
(v) 500 Rifle Grenades
(vi) 5,000 sandbags.
(vii) Spare tools.

16. Prisoners will be sent down to X.28.b.2.6., men of the 10/11th High.L.I. companies in support being used for this purpose. Receipts will be obtained.

17. **Correct time**
Every unit in the Brigade, including the 73rd Field Coy. R.E. and Company 9th Gordons (Pioneers) attached will send an officer to Brigade Headquarters at 12.30 p.m. to-morrow to receive the correct time.

18. (a) Advanced Headquarters, 12th High.L.I. for the purpose of this operation will be situated in 6th AVENUE just W. of BOYAU connecting 6th AVENUE with front line (S.1.d.5.2½.)

O.C. Brigade Signal Section will arrange to connect him with Brigade Headquarters and the battalions of his right and left.

(b) Staff Officer of the 46th Inf. Bde. will be attached to H.Q., 12th High.L.I. for the sole purpose of transmitting information.

(c) Brigade Headquarters will be in its present positions in SHELTER WOOD to where all reports will be sent.

[signature]
Captain,
Bde Maj.,
46th Inf.Bde.

Issued at 5. S/m
through Signals.

Copy No		
1.	File
2	War Diary
3	7/8th K.O.Sco.Bord.
4	10th Sco.Rif.
5	10/11th High.L.I.
6	12th High.L.I.
7	46th M.G. Company
8	46th T.M.Battery
9	Staff Captain
10	Brigade Signalling Off.
11	73rd Field Coy.R.E.
12	O.C., "G" Coy, 9th Gordons
13	Medium T.M.Battery
14	179th Tunnelling Coy.R.E.
15	44th Inf.Bde.
16	45th Inf.Bde.
17	112th Inf.Bde.
18	15th Division.
19	Spare
20	Spare.

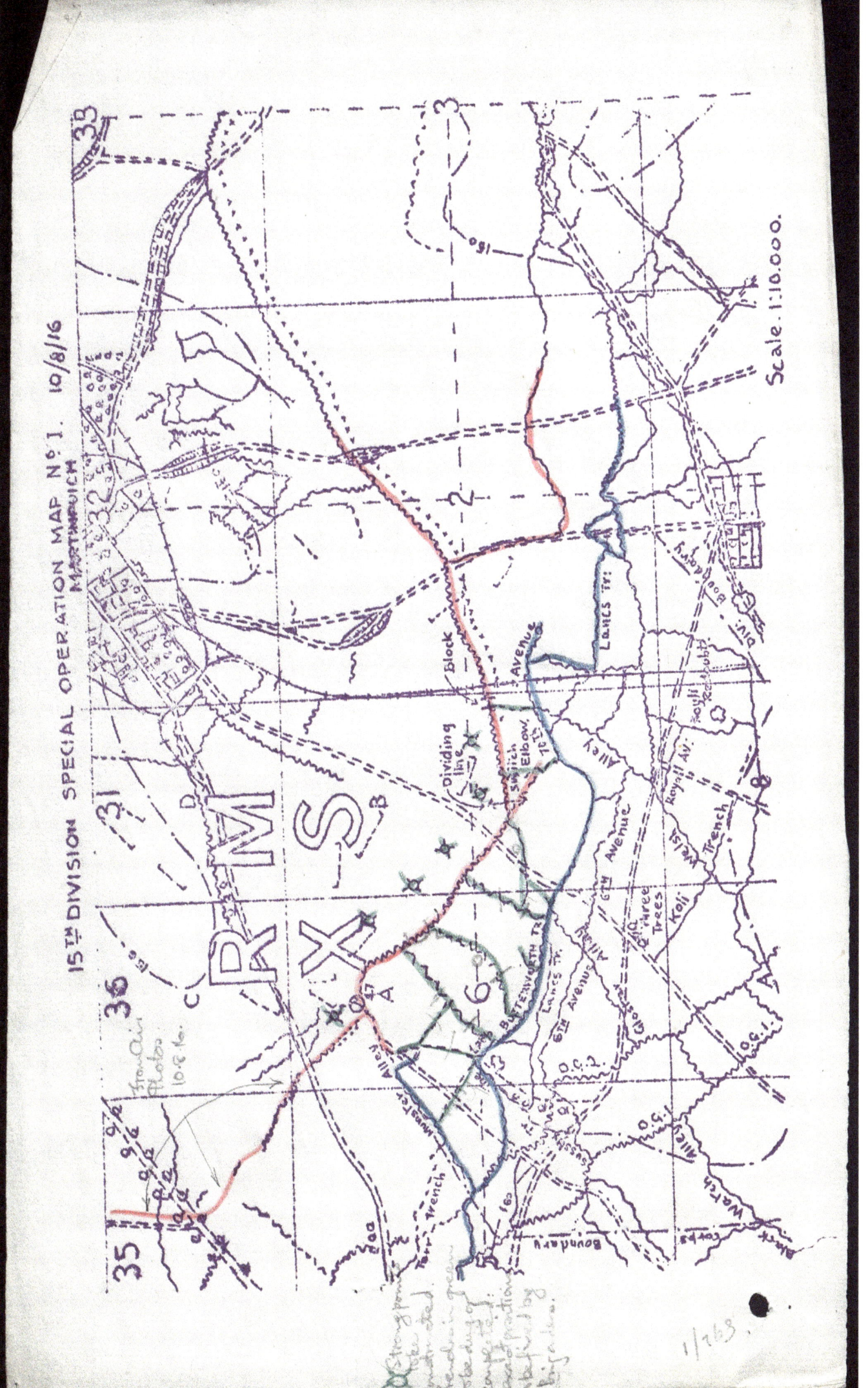

S E C R E T. 　　　C O P Y NO. 9

**HEADQUARTERS.
15th DIVISION.
1. AUG. 1916**

45TH INFANTRY BRIGADE OPERATION ORDER NO. 104.

Brigade Headquarters,
12th August 1916.

Reference:-
Special Operation Map attached. — *Not attached word for* ...

1. On the night August 12th/13th the 15th Division will attack the enemy SWITCH LINE from S.1.d.9.9. to point 47 in X.6.a. (MUNSTER ALLEY).

2. The 4th Australian Division have been asked to assist by forming a defensive flank on the left of the attack.
ZERO hour will be communicated later.

3. The 45th Infantry Brigade will attack on the left the 46th Infantry Brigade on the Right.
Dividing line between Brigades 30 yards East of junction of GLOSTER ALLEY with SWITCH LINE.

4. The attack by the 45th Infantry Brigade will be carried out by the 6/7th R. Scots Fusiliers and the 6th Cameron Highlanders. The 6/7th R. S. Fusiliers will be on the right, the 6th Cameron Highrs on the left.

5. On the 12th August the Heavy Artillery will bombard the GERMAN SWITCH LINE from 10 a.m. to 1 p.m., during which period GLOSTER ALLEY Sap and MUNSTER ALLEY Sap will be evacuated.

6. On the 12th instant, the 6th Cameron Highlanders will relieve the 13th Royal Scots in the front line under arrangements to be made by O's. C. concerned.
The relief will not commence before 6.30 a.m., and will be completed by 10 a.m.

7. At 6 p.m. on the 12th instant, the O. C. 6th Cameron Highrs. will commence closing his battalion to the left, and at the same hour the O. C. 6/7th R. Scots Fusiliers will fill the gaps so caused by moving up his battalion by platoons.
The dividing line between battalions will be the sap at the U of BUTTERWORTH inclusive to the 6/7th R. Scots Fusiliers.
The Right of the 6/7th R. S. Fusiliers will rest on the CONTALMAISON - MARTINPUICH ROAD. The left of the 6th Cameron Highrs. will rest on MUNSTER ALLEY.

8. At 7 p.m. on the 12th instant, the O. C. 11th A & S. Highrs. will start moving his battalion by platoons in position as under:-
2 Companies into GOULAY TRENCH.
2   "   less 1 platoon into CONTALMAISON.
1 platoon with 1 Lewis Gun into Strong Point at CONTALMAISON VILLA.
Headquarters. CONTALMAISON.

9. At 8 p.m. on the 12th instant, the O. C. 13th Royal Scots will move 2 companies to CONTALMAISON and will garrison the Strong posts at the CUTTING and at the N. W. of the Village, each with a platoon and one Lewis gun.

10. The frontage to be attacked is approximately 650 yards. The objective being closer to the right of our attack than the left, a line will be marked with tape parallel to the objective and approximately 150 yards from it under the direction of the O.C. 73rd Field Coy. R. E.

(2).

11. On the night of the 12th/13th, 15 minutes before ZERO the normal barrage will be brought on to the trenches to be attacked. At ZERO HOUR the objective will be subjected to an intense bombardment.
   The fire will lift at the following times:-
   0.2. Lift 100 yards.
   0.3. Lift 50 yards.
   0.5. Lift 50 yards.
   0.7. Lift 50 yards.

12. At ZERO hour the 6/7th R. Scots Fusiliers and 6th Cameron Highrs. will be disposed as under 150 yards from the enemy trench:-
   First Wave - 6 platoons of each battalion.)
   Second " - 6 platoons of each battalion.) 6 companies.
   Two platoons of each company in the first wave being supported by 2 platoons of the same company in the second wave.
   1 Company each the 6/7th R. Scots Fusiliers and 6th Cameron Highrs. in support will move into the front line as vacated by the first and second waves.
   Lewis guns will accompany their companies.

13. At ZERO HOUR the Infantry will advance and will assault close under the artillery barrage.

14. The position will be consolidated as follows:-
   (a). A strong point will be established immediately South of the figure 4 in Point 47 to protect the left.
   (b). Three strong points will be established to the N.E. of the captured SWITCH LINE.
   (c). The captured line will be connected up with GLOSTER ALLEY & MUNSTER ALLEY, and an intermediate communication trench will be dug
   (d). The SWITCH LINE will be consolidated by digging a new trench immediately in rear of it.
   Infantry patrols will be pushed out at least 100 yards to cover the construction of the strong points.
   The 6/7th R. Scots Fusiliers and 6th Cameron Highlanders will each be responsible for the construction of the two strong points on their front.
   These strong points will be occupied by Lewis and Vickers guns.

15. The O. C. 6th Cameron Highlanders will detail bombing and blocking parties to deal with the hostile trench that enters MUNSTER ALLEY at about the Y of MUNSTER ALLEY.

16. The O. C. 45th M. G. Coy. will detail a section to be placed at the disposal of each of the two assaulting battalions.

17. O's. C. Medium and Stokes T. M. Batteries will arrange to cover the left flank of the attack.

18. Two platoons 9th Gordon Highlanders (Pioneers) will be employed connecting the SWITCH LINE with the present front line by continuing the sap from the U of BUTTERWORTH. They will be assembled in the new communication from GOULAY TRENCH to O. G. 1., but will not move up until ordered by either the O. C. 6/7th R. Scots Fusiliers or O .C. 6th Cameron Highlanders.

19. No bombing will be employed along the SWITCH ELBOW to the East of junction of GLOSTER SAP with the SWITCH. Connection will be established as soon as possible with the 46th Infantry Brigade.

20. Every man will carry 220 rounds of S.A.A.

21. 50% will carry tools, in the proportion of one pick to 4 shovels. This includes all waves and the company in support.

22. 4 sandbags per man will be carried.

23. Arrangements for rations, water, supply of bombs and S.A.A., have been issued separately.

(3).

24. Dumps of stores have been established at:-

BOMBS.
(a). 120 yards E. of junction of MUNSTER ALLEY & O.G. 2.
(b). 20 yards E. of junction of 6th AVENUE & GLOSTER ALLEY.

S.A.A.
(a). Junction of GLOSTER ALLEY & BUTTERWORTH TRENCH.
(b). Junction of GLOSTER ALLEY & O.G. 2.
(c). Junction MUNSTER ALLEY & O.G. 2.

WATER.
Junction of GLOSTER ALLEY & O.G. 2.

A carrying party of 1 Officer and 25 men from 13th Royal Scots will be placed at the disposal of O's. C. 6/7th R. Scots Fusiliers and 6th Cameron Highlanders, who will notify O. C. 13th Royal Scots the time and where these parties are required.

25. Watches will be synchronised at 5 p.m. on the 12th instant at 46th Infantry Brigade Headquarters.

26. A contact aeroplane patrol will fly over the objective at 6 a.m. 13th instant. It will sound a KLAXON horn, and the advanced line of Infantry will then display flares at the bottom of the trenches.

Laurence Carr

Major.,

Brigade Major, 45th Infantry Brigade.

Issued at   a.m.
All recipients of O. Orders.
Copy No. 12. 15th Div. "Q".
         13. 46th Inf. Bde.
         14. 12th Australian I. B.
         15. 73rd R. E.
         16. 9th Gordon Highlanders. (Pioneers).

"A" Form.
MESSAGES AND SIGNALS.

Prefix	Code	m.	Words	Charge	This message is on a/c of:		Recd. at
Office of Origin and Service Instructions.						Service.	Date
SECRET			Sent At ___ m. To By		(Signature of "Franking Officer.")		From By

TO { 45 Inf Bde   34 Divn
     46 Inf Bde

Sender's Number.	Day of Month	In reply to Number	AAA

G 944 12.

Heavy Arty (III rd Corps) are bombarding the enemy's entrenched line from S21d6 to S2c85 and the communication trench running East from the intersection line from S2c85 to S2c88 between 12 noon and 3pm to-day. After 3pm till dark the 4·5" Howitzers will be firing on the Uncovered after dark 18pdrs MMM. It will be necessary to evacuate trenches within a radius of 200 yards from Pt S2c85 between 12 noon and 3pm and within a radius of 50 yards after the latter hour MM Acknowledge by wire.

From
Place 15" Divn
Time

SECRET.

HEADQUARTERS,
15th DIVISION.
7 AUG. 1916
G.408.

Hd. Qrs. 15th Division.
C.R.A. 1st Division (for information).

3rd Corps H.A.
27th H.A.G.

1. The Heavy Artillery (IIIrd Corps) are bombarding the enemy's intermediate line from S.2.d.0.6. to S.2.c.8.5. and the communication trench running North from the Intermediate line from S.2.c.8.5. to S.2.c.8.8. between 12 noon and 3 p.m. to-morrow. After 3 p.m. till dark the 4.5" howitzers will be firing on this area and after dark 18 pounders.

2. Can you please arrange to evacuate your trenches within a radius of 200 yards from Pt. S.2.c.8.5. between 12 noon and 3 p.m. and a within radius of 50 yards after the latter hour.

3. The 112th Inf. Brigade are attacking the intermediate line at Zero hour to-morrow night. A direct attack on this line has been arranged and therefore facilities for forming up in your area will not now be required.

I am much obliged to you for having offered me facilities for forming up in LANCASHIRE TRENCH had I found such a course n necessary.

4 Please acknowledge

Major-General,
Commanding 34th Division.

11-8-16.

45th Infy Bde
725/G.

HEADQUARTERS,
15th DIVISION.
11 AUG 1916
Reg. No. 1779

15 Division

Reference Telephone conversation and your Secret No 100(A)/4 G-2. para 3 –

I am of opinion that it will be quite possible to take & consolidate the SWITCH as ordered provided I am permitted to throw back the alignment of the strong points on my left near point 47 on your special operation Map No 1 dated 10.8.16 – This I understand has the sanction of the G.O.C –

M Sangood
B. General
45th Bde

11-VIII.-16

"A" Form.
Army Form C. 2121.
MESSAGES AND SIGNALS.

HEADQUARTERS,
5th DIVISION
12 AUG 1916

SECRET

TO 46th Inf Bde

Sender's Number: G954
Day of Month: 12th Aug
AAA

3rd Div now say that they will attack direct on intermediate line at Zero hour tonight and consequently they will not require to take over the right hand portion of your line

From: 15 Div
Time: 10 A

SECRET.

15th Division.
No.100/5/5 G.a.

45th Inf. Bde.
46th Inf. Bde.

Herewith Copy No. X R.A. 23rd Divn. Order No.27 together with tables of bombardments in connection with operations tomorrow night.

Major, G.S.

12th Aug/16.   15th Division.

SECRET.

S/1/84.

HEADQUARTERS
15th DIVISION

AUG 1916

Ref. No. 1980

COPY NO: 1

R.A. 23rd Division Order No: 57.

Reference: (Sketch issued.
(and Special Operation Map No: 1.   11th August, 1916.

1. (a) 4th Australian Division on night 12th/13th August is attacking on the line R.34.a.8.3. - 6.5 - 0.3 - R.33.b.5.5. - 3.2.

    (b) On the night August 12th/13th the 15th Division will attack the enemy's switch line from S.1.d.9.9. to point 47 in X.3.a. (MUNSTER ALLEY).
    The 4th Australian Division have been asked to assist by forming a defensive flank on the left of the attack.
    Zero time will be communicated later.

    (c) The 46th Infantry Brigade is attacking on the right, the 45th Infantry Brigade on the left. Dividing line between Brigades 30 yards E. of junction of GLOSTER ALLEY with switch line (SWITCH ELBOW).

2. (a) At zero our Infantry will be formed up 150 yards from the switch trench; at zero they advance and assault close under our barrage.

    (b) The position will be consolidated, a double block formed on the right, and a series of strong points established not more than 100 yards in front of captured trench, covering parties being pushed out close under the barrage during their construction.

3. Artillery co-operation is as follows:-

    (a) Heavy Artillery. Communications, strong points, etc, North of the switch line and Counter-Battery work.

    (b) Right Flank Barrage. 1st Divisional Artillery.

    (c) Left Flank Barrage. 34th Divisional Artillery.

    (d) Main Barrage. 23rd Divisional Artillery including 175th and 176th Brigades.
    A detailed programme of this is attached.

4. Liaison arrangements will be as at present.

5. Watches will be synchronized at the 46th Infantry Brigade Head Qtrs: SHELTER WOOD at 5 p.m. on the 12th instant.
    An officer of each Artillery Brigade will be present.

6. ACKNOWLEDGE.

A. K. Hay.
Major,

Issued at 11.50 p.m.   Brigade Major R.A. 23rd Division.

Copies Nos: 1 to 5 15th Division.   25 - 29 105th Bde: R.F.A.
            6 R.A. 3rd Corps.   30 - 34 175th "   "
            7 R.A. 1st Division.   35 - 40 176th Bde: R.F.A.
            8 R.A. 34th Divn: 41 & 42 Liaison Officer 45th
            9 LAHORE Artillery.   Brigade.
            10 to 14 102nd Bde: R.F.A.   43 - 45 Liaison Officer 46th
            15 to 19 103rd   "   "   46 & 47 Dismth Brigade.
            20 - 24 104th Bde: R.F.A.   48 Staff Captain R.A.

LIFTS.

HOUR	UNIT	OBJECTIVE	RATE	AMMN:	REMARKS.
At 0.2. (1st Lift)	175th Bde: 104th Bde: 105th Bde:	Lift 100 yards to the North.			At 0.2. All Howitzers and 18 Prs: on the communication in rear remain on their targets and do not lift.
	176th Bde: 102nd Bde: 103rd Bde: Sectn: 46th Bty:	Lift 100 yards to the North East.	From 0.3 to 0.7. 18 Prs: Six rounds per gun per minute. Hows: Two rounds per gun per minute.	SHRAPNEL. 18 Prs: H.E. Hows:	At 0.3. Howitzers of 176th Bde: lift on to Railway about M.31.d.5.3½. Hows: of 102nd Bde: lift on to Trench Junos: about M.31.d.7.5. Hows: of a 103rd Bde: concentrate on road at M.31.d.8.4.
At 0.3 (2nd Lift)	175th Bde: 104th Bde: 105th Bde:	Lift 50 yards to the North.			
	176th Bde: 102nd Bde: 103rd Bde: Sectn: 46th Bty:	Lift 50 yards to the North East.			
At 0.5. (3rd Lift)	175th Bde: 104th Bde: 105th Bde:	Lift 50 yards to the North.	From 0.7 to 0.10. 18 Prs: Four rounds per gun per minute. Hows: Two rounds per gun per minute.		
	176th Bde: 102nd Bde: 103rd Bde: Sectn: 46th Bty:	Lift 50 yards to the North East.			
At 0.7. (4th Lift)	175th Bde: 104th Bde: 105th Bde:	Lift 50 yards to the North.			This barrage continued till 0.10.
	176th Bde: 102nd Bde: 103rd Bde: Sectn: 43th Bty:	Lift 50 yards to the North East.			

NOTE. From 0.2 to 0.10, 175th Bde: will keep one 18 pounder Battery on Switch line from S.2.a.8.1. to S.2.a.4.2½. Its other two Batteries will lift as per Table.

FINAL BARRAGE.

HOUR	UNIT	OBJECTIVES	RATE	AMMUNITION	REMARKS.
From 0.10 onwards.	175th Bde:	Along road S.2.a.6.1. to S.2.a.3.6.	0.10 to 1.0. 18 Prs: 3 rounds per gun per minute. Hows: 1 round per gun per 2 minutes.	18 Prs: Shrapnel from 0.10 to 1.0. After 1.0 - 3 Shrapnel to 1 H.E. Hows: H.E.	Howitzers still on point S.2.a.6.1.
	104th Bde:	S.2.a.3.6. to S.2.a.0.5.	1.0 to 2.0. 18 Prs: 1 rd: per gun per min: Hows: 1 rd: per gun per 3 mins:		Howitzers and 1 18 Pr: gun still on railway S.2.a.0.7. to M.32.c.2.2.
	105th Bde:	S.2.a.0.5. to S.1.b.6.4.	2.0 onwards. 18 Prs: 1 rd: per gun per 2 minutes. Hows: 1 rd: per gun per 4 mins:		Howitzers still on trench S.1.b.6.5. to M.31.d.8.2. One Section 18 Prs: still on road S.1.b.7.6. to M.31.d.9.1.
	173rd Bde:	S.1.b.6.4. to S.1.b.3.8.			Howitzers still on railway about M.31.d.5.3½.
	102nd Bde:	S.1.b.3.8. to M.31.d.2.0.			Howitzers still on trench junctions about M.31.d.7.5.
	103rd Bde:	M.31.d.2.0. to M.31.d.0.3.			Howitzers still on road at M.31.d.6.4.
	Section 46th Battery.	S.1.b.6.4. to M.31.d.0.3.			

B O M B A R D M E N T.

HOUR	UNIT	OBJECTIVE	RATE	AMMUNITN:	REMARKS.
- 15 to ZERO	175th Bde:	Switch line S.2.a.6.1. to S.2.c.0.9.	1 round per gun per 5 minutes. {18 Prs {Hows:	18 Prs: SHRAPNEL. Hows: H. E.	Howitzers on point S.2.a.6.1. 1 18 Pr: Section on road S.2.a. 3.5. to M.32.c.4.2.
2 minutes.	104th Bde:	Switch line S.2.c.0.9. to road at S.1.d.2½.0.			Howitzers on railway from S.2.a.0.7. to K.32.c.2.2. - also one 18 Pr: gun.
2 ↓	105th Bde:	Switch line S.2.c.0.9. to road at S.1.d.2½.9.	ZERO to + 2 18 Prs: 6 rounds per gun per minute. Hows: 2 rounds per gun per minute.		Howitzers on trench S.1.b.6.6. to M.31.d.8.2. One Section 18 Prs: on road S.1.b.7.6. to M.31.d.9.1.
to	176th Bde:	Switch line S.2.c.3.8. to X.6.a.9.1½.			Howitzers on old Battery Position about S.1.b.1½.6½.
15 minutes	102nd Bde:	Switch line S.1.b.0.1. to X.6.a.7.4½.			Howitzers on old Battery Position about X.6.a.8.6.
	103rd Bde:	Switch Line X.6.a.7½.4. to X.6.a.4.7.			Howitzers on road H.36.c.8½.0. to H.31.d.6.4. - 1 Section 18 Prs: on road H.31.d.0.1. to H.31.d.6.4.
-	Section 43th Bty:	Enfilade switch line from S.1.d.3.8. to X.6.a.4.7.			

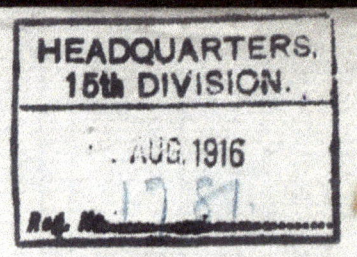

AMENDMENT TO 46th Infantry Brigade
ORDER No. 84.

In para 17 of 46th Infantry Brigade
Order No. 84 dated 11th August -

For "12.30 p.m." read "5 p.m."

Acknowledge.

Brigade Headquarters,
11th August, 1916.

Captain,
Bde. Major,
46th Inf. Bde.

Issued to all recipients of 46th Infantry Brigade
Order No. 84.

SECRET.

S/1/83-4.

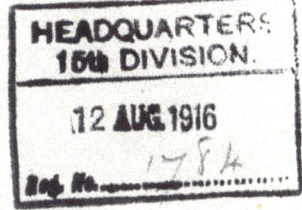
HEADQUARTERS
15th DIVISION.
12 AUG 1916
Ref No. 1784

COPY NO: 1

The attached Table is issued in continuation of this office S/1/83 of 10th, and S/1/83-2 of 11th August.

ACKNOWLEDGE.

R.K.Hall
Major,

Issued at 8.30 a.m.   Brigade Major R.A. 23rd Divn:

Copies to

    15th Division   103rd Bde: R.F.A.
    R.A. 3rd Corps.   104th   "   "
    LAHORE Artillery. 105th   "   "
    34th Divn: Arty: 175th   "   "
    1st Divn: Arty: 25th   "   "
    102nd Bde: R.F.A. Diary.

Copies No 1 and 5 retained
Copy No 2 to 44 Inf Bde
     3 " 45 " "
     4 " 46 " "

           9.30 AM

NINTH and LAST RELIEF.
From 2 p.m. 12th August to 10.15 p.m. 12th August.

UNIT	OBJECTIVES	RATE	AMMUNITION	REMARKS.
D/25	Block switch trench at about S.2.a.6.2.	1 Round per gun per 5 minutes.	H.E.	
D/103	Block switch trench at X.6.a.4.7.			
103rd Bde: (less D/103)	Switch line X.6.a.4.7. to S.1.b.0.1.	1 Round per gun per 4 minutes.	SHRAPNEL to H.E.	From 5.30 to 6 p.m. 104th and 175th Bdes: will drop barrage on to the switch line itself on the Infantry have been warned of this. At 2.30 p.m.) Increase rate of fire At 4.10 p.m.) to 1 round At 7.15 p.m.) per gun per 2 At 8.55 p.m.) minutes. Lift 100 yards behind switch line — after 2 minutes lift another 50, then area. 3 minutes lift another 50 – then drop back after 3 minutes to the original barrage, at normal rate.
104th Bde: (less D/104)	S.1.b.0.1. to S.2.a.0.1. also 1 gun on track X.6.a.4.7. to MARTINPUICH. 1 gun on track and trench S.1.b.5.6. to MARTINPUICH. 1 gun on railway S.2.a.0.2. to MARTINPUICH.			
175th Bde:	S.2.a.0.1. to S.2.a.6.1. – also 1 gun on road S.2.a.5.6. to MARTINPUICH.			

SECRET.

n15th Division No. 100(3)/4 G.a.

Reference 15th Division Operation Order No. 73 para. 2.

ZERO TIME will be - 10.30 p.m.

Sgd. L. Henderson Major
for
Lieut. Colonel,

11th Aug., 1916.   General Staff, 15th Division.

Copies to:-
  III Corps.
  III Corps H.Arty.
  34th Div.
  4th Australian Div.
  44th Inf. Bde.
  45th Inf. Bde.
  46th Inf. Bde.
  9th Gordons.
  15th Signals.
  A.D.M.S.
  A.P.M.
  "A" & "Q".
  15th D.A.
  C.R.E.
  23rd D.A.

SECRET.

Copy No. 6

ADDENDUM NO. 1

to

III CORPS OPERATION ORDER NO. 108.   11/8/16.

....

Reference Para. 2.

ZERO TIME will be: 10.30 p.m.

Acknowledge on attached slip.

....

Issued by D.R. at 12.30 p.m.
To all recipients of O.O. No. 108.
Telephoned by code to 15th. Divn.
     at 11.45 a.m.

for Brigadier-General,
General Staff,
III Corps.

\# Sent by D.R. to all recipients
of O.O. Zero time 10.30

45th Infantry Brigade No. 717/G.

13th Royal Scots.
6/7th R. Scots Fusiliers.
6th Cameron Highlanders.
11th A & S. Highlanders.
45th M. G. Coy.
45th T. M. Battery.
15th Division.
46th Infantry Brigade.
12th Aust. I. B.

1. In order to determine whether the GERMAN SWITCH LINE from SWITCH ELBOW to its junction with MUNSTER ALLEY is occupied by the enemy, 4 officers patrols will reconnoitre this line to-night the 11th/12th August.

2. The artillery barrage will be as follows:-

   10 p.m. Normal barrage on SWITCH LINE, lifts 100 yards.
  10.5 p.m. Lifts 100 yards.
  10.6 p.m. Lifts 50 yards.
  10.8 p.m. Lifts 50 yards and continues on this line.

3. In the event of the SWITCH LINE being found unoccupied, working parties will move forward and establish 4 strong points at about:-

       X. 6. a. 3. 8.
       X. 6. a. 9. 6.
       S. 1. b. ½. 4.
       S. 1. b. 2. 1.

These working parties will be ready to move forward on receipt of a message from the patrols that all is clear.

The patrols in this case will act as covering party.

4. If any opposition is met by any of the patrols, the whole operations will be abandoned.

11/8/16.

Brigade Major, 45th Infantry Brigade.

SECRET.

15th Division No. 100(6)/4 G.a.

45th Inf. B^de.
─────────────

I attach a copy of a letter received from the G.O.C. 4th Australian Division this evening and of the reply of the G.O.C. Division to it.

This confirms the telephone conversation of 7.30 p.m. to-day at which it was arranged that you should protect your left flank.

You will continue in close touch with the 12th Australian Infantry Brigade.

H Knox
Lieut. Colonel,
11th Aug., 1916.   General Staff, 15th Division.

SECRET.

15th Division No. 100(5)/4 G.a.

4th Australian Division.
_____

Your G.5/57 dated 11.8.16.
_____

1.I am much obliged for your proposals which will materially assist my operations.

2.Reconnaissance has shown that the enemy has a trench joining MUNSTER ALLEY from the north about X.6.a.3.6. and that the German Switch about X.6.a.4.7. has been obliterated.

I have consequently decided to round off the salient in X.6.a. by placing the strong point at about X.6.a.3.6. instead of at X.6.a.4.8. as was indicated in the special Operation Order Map No. 1.

3.My Brigadier General Commanding 45th Infantry Brigade is in close touch with your 12th Australian Brigade.

Major General,
11th August, 1916.Commanding, 15th (Scottish) Division.

S E C R E T.
U R G E N T.

No. G. 5/57

Headquarters,
4th. AUSTRALIAN DIVISION.
11th. AUGUST, 1916.

Headquarters,
15th. Division.

Reference 15th. Division Order Number 73.

The 12th. Aus. Infantry Brigade on the right of this Division has built four strong points, as per attached sketch. These should be completed by tomorrow morning, and I am instructing G.O.C. 12th. Aus. Infantry Brigade to occupy these strong points and to cover your left flank during your advance.

Please say if you agree to these dispositions.

I would suggest that G.O.C. your left Brigade should get into touch with G.O.C. 12th. Aus. Infantry Brigade, to ensure close co-operation between them.

Major-General.
Comdg. 4th. AUSTRALIAN DIVISION.

S E C R E T.

15th Division No. 100 (1)/4.
G.a.

III Corps.
III Corps H.Art.
34th Div.
4th Australian Div.
44th Inf. Bde.
45th Inf. Bde.
46th Inf. Bde.
23rd Div. Art.
15th Signals.

---

1. In para. 11 of 15th Division Operation Order No. 73 for "12 noon" read "5 p.m.".

2. ACKNOWLEDGE.

Not k
III Corps
34 Div
Aus. Div

K Henderson Major

Lieut. Colonel,
General Staff, 15th Division.

11th Aug., 1916.

SECRET.

Copy No. 7

ADDENDUM NO. 1

to

III CORPS OPERATION ORDER NO. 108.   11/8/16.

....

Reference Para. 2.,

ZERO TIME will be: 10.30 p.m.

Acknowledge on attached slip.

....

Issued by D.R. at 12.30 p.m.

To all recipients of O.O. No. 108.

Telephoned by code to 15th. Divn.
at 11.45 a.m.

for Brigadier-General,
General Staff,
III Corps.

URGENT & SECRET.

S/1/83-3.

15th Division.
R.A. 34th Division.
O.C. 102nd Bde: R.F.A.
O.C. 103rd "   "
O.C. 104th "   "
O.C. 105th "   "
O.C. 175th "   "
O.C. 25th :

With reference to my S/1/83-2 of to-day giving details of the SIXTH RELIEF tonight, i.e. from 8 p.m. 11th August to 2 a.m. 12th August -

1. The 45th Brigade (left) will send patrols out tonight to the switch line between X.6.a.4.7. and the road at S.1.d.2½.9. at 10 p.m. If the enemy trench is found to be unoccupied, they will seize and consolidate it straight away. If it is found to be held they will withdraw after reconnaissance.

2. This operation necessitates the following alterations to SIXTH RELIEF and also possibly to SEVENTH RELIEF:-

   <u>34th Div: Artillery.</u> At 10 p.m. to lift their fire and place a barrage on the railway from R.36.c.4.0. to M.31.d.0.2½, and to maintain this until informed by this office that it may come back to the original barrage.

   <u>D/104.</u> To stop firing at 10 p.m. until ordered to re-open.

   25th Bde: }
   Section 46th Bty: } Will carry out the following programme, 105th
   Part of 105th Bde) Bde: lifting only that part of their fire which is W. of the point S.1.b.5.1.

   At 10 p.m. fire will be lifted 100 yards behind the Switch line, that is to the N.E.

   At 10.5 p.m. it will lift another 100 yards to the N.E.

   At 10.6 p.m. it will lift another 50 yards to the N.E.

   At 10.8 p.m. it will lift another 50 yards to the N.E. and will remain here (that is 300 yards behind Switch line) until ordered to return to original barrage by this office.

3. Should the SEVENTH RELIEF have received no further orders from this office they will take it that our infantry are still in the Switch trench, in which case 103rd Bde: and that part of 104th Bde: W. of point S.1.b.5.1. will open at 2 a.m. on a barrage 300x N.E. of Switch trench instead of on the trench itself. D/103 will not open fire till ordered.

4. Patrols from the Right Brigade (46th) are going out to reconnoitre only between 11.50 p.m. and 1.20 a.m., as originally ordered in the Table for SIXTH RELIEF, and during these hours all units firing on or behind Switch line E. of the point S.1.b.5.1. will lift 300 yards to the North whilst these patrols are out, returning to original barrage at 1.20 a.m.

5. ACKNOWLEDGE. by wire.

A. K. Hay.
Major,
Brigade Major R.A. 23rd Division.

11th August, 1916.

SECRET.

SECRET.

15th Division No. 100(4)/4 G.a.

45th Inf. Bde.
_____

1.   Your G.718 and previous reconnaissance reports received today.
     The G.O.C. is very pleased with the excellent work performed.

2.   With regard to your request that the road and railway on your north flank should be dealt with. I have this afternoon been to the Corps with your report and the Corps will arrange that the road and railway are kept under a barrage while your operations on the 12th/13th are in progress. They will deal with the railway from a point about 200 yards east of the old German second line.
     It will also be necessary to arrange to guard this flank as you explained to the G.O.C. you are proposing to do. The new trench coming from the North into MUNSTER ALLEY will also require watching.

3.   Is it to be understood that you do not consider this sufficient and that you think the railway must be attacked, if the operation against the Switch is to be successful? The 4th Australian Division cannot undertake this nor is the G.O.C. clear that the Corps Commander would wish us to push out so far at this stage.

                                              (signature)
                                              Lieut. Colonel,
11th Aug., 1916.   General Staff, 15th Division.

"A" Form.
MESSAGES AND SIGNALS.
Army Form C. 2121.

TO: 15 Division

Sender's Number: G 718. Day of Month: -11- AAA

I forward herewith another report from an Officers patrol 11th A & S.H. which proceeded last night at about 11 P.m. up MUNSTER ALLEY. —

This patrol substantiates other reports & goes to show that although THE SWITCH may not be occupied at all, that the Road, Railway which runs parallel to MUNSTER ALLEY on its north west side is still held —

Should this be the case any enterprise on the SWITCH will be enfiladed and taken in flank from there. As I do not see how the ANZACS can form a defensive flank which can be of any use, I suggest that steps may be taken on night of Aug 12th.

"A" Form.
MESSAGES AND SIGNALS.

Army Form C. 2121.

to ensure that no hostile fire can
interfere with our operations on the
SWITCH from this direction.
I have seen the officers who carried
out the patrol & am positive that
an advance to consolidate our position
along the line of the SWITCH must
be assisted by an advance on the left
of MUNSTER ALLEY. And that the new
trench mentioned in the attached report
be investigated —

From 45th Bde

(Z) W? August B?

45th Bde

S E C R E T.

15th Division No. 100/4 G.a.

44th Inf. Bde.
45th Inf. Bde.
46th Inf. Bde.
9th Gordons.
23rd Divl. Arty.
4th Australian Division.

Reference 15th Division No. 100 (2)/4 G.a. of 10.8.16., para. 1 (ii).

To admit of a reconnaissance being made tonight of the German SWITCH LINE in X.6.A. the normal barrage maintained on and in rear of that line will be lifted as follows :-

11.8.16.	10 p.m. lift	100 yards.
"	10.6 p.m. "	100	"
"	10.6 p.m. "	50	"
"	10.8 p.m. "	50	"

At 10.8 a box barrage will be formed - right on MARTINPUICH - CONTALMAISON Road, Left on Railway R.36.c.4.0. to M.31.d.0.8½. connected by a line 300 yards from and on the North Eastern side of the German SWITCH LINE.

The 45th Infantry Brigade will inform Headquarters 23rd Divl. R.A. when the barrage is to drop to its normal line.

2. The previous arrangement to lift the barrage behind this portion of the SWITCH LINE from 11.50 p.m to 1.20 a.m. is cancelled, but still holds good with regard to the barrage East of the MARTINPUICH - CONTALMAISON Road.

Lieut. Colonel,

11th Aug., 1916.   General Staff, 15th Division.

SECRET.

S/1/83-2.

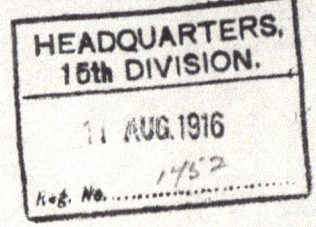
HEADQUARTERS,
15th DIVISION.
11 AUG.1916
Reg. No. 1752

COPY NO: ....

10th August, 1913.

The attached Tables are forwarded in continuation of this office letter No: S/1/83 (Secret) of 10th instant.

ACKNOWLEDGE.

Issued at 8.30 p.m.

A. K. Hay.
Major,
Brigade Major R.A. 23rd Division.

Copies to:-

15th Division.
R.A. IIIrd Corps.
Lahore Artilery.
34th Divn: Artillery.
1st Divn: Artillery.
102nd Bde: R.F.A.
103rd   "   "
104th   "   "
105th   "   "
175th   "   "
25th   "   "
Diary.

*Copy No 1 retained.
2 to 44 Bde
3 .. 45 ..
4 .. 46 ..*

SECRET.

S/1/83-2.
1752

Fifth RELIEF.

From 2 p.m. 11th August to 8 p.m. 11th August.

UNIT	OBJECTIVES	RATE	PROJECTILE.	REMARKS.
D/25	Block Switch Trench at about S.2.a.6.2.	1 Round per gun per 5 minutes	H.E.	
/103	Block Switch Trench at X.6.a.4.7.			
13rd Bde: less D/103)	Switch Line X.6.a.4.7. to S.1.b.0.1.	1 Round per gun per 5 minutes	5 Shrapnel ? / H.E	At 2.50 p.m.) Search slowly back behind 3.45 p.m.) Switch Line in 50 yard 5.0 p.m.) searches for 600 yards - 5.10 p.m.) remaining at each range 7.20 p.m.) for 1 minute and increasing rate to 1 round per gun per minute all shrapnel. After reaching 600 yards behind Switch Line, drop suddenly back to original barrage at normal rate of fire.
4th Bde: less D/104)	S.1.b.0.1. to S.2.c.0.1. also 1 gun on track X.8.a.4.7. to HARTIMPUICH. 1 gun on track and trench S.1.b.C.6. to HARTIMPUICH. 1 gun on railway S.2.a.0.2. to HARTIMPUICH.			
9th Bde:	S.2.a.0.1. to S.2.a.8.1. also 1 gun on road S.2.a.3.6. to HARTIMPUICH.			From 2 to 2.30 p.m. and from 7.45 to 8 p.m. 104th and 175th Bdes: will drop their barrage on to the actual switch trench itself, that is from S.1.b.0.1. thro' point S.1.d.3.8. to S.2.c.0.9. for 104th Bde:, and from S.2.c.0.9. to S.2.a.6.1. for 175th Bde: Infantry are being warned of this.

SIXTH RELIEF.
From 8 p.m. 11th August to 2 a.m. 12th August.

UNIT	OBJECTIVE	RATE	PROJECTILE	REMARKS.
D/102	Block Switch Trench at about S.2.a.5.2.	1 Round per gun per 3 minutes.	H.E.	Stop firing from 11.50 p.m. to 1.20 a.m. when patrols are out.
D/104	Block Switch Trench at X.6.a.4.7.			
1 Section 46th Batty:	Infilade Switch Trench from S.1.b.0.1. to X.6.a.4.7.	1 Round per gun per 2 minutes.	5 Shrapnel to 1 H.E.	From 1.45 a.m. to 2 a.m. 105th Brigade will drop their barrage on to Switch trench itself from S.1.b.0.1. thro' point S.2.c.0.3.8. to S.2.c.0.9. - 102nd Bde: will also drop on to Switch line from S.2.c.0.9. to S.2.a.3.1. Infantry are being warned.
25th Bde: (less D/25)	Switch trench from S.1.b.0.1. to X.5.a.4.7.			
105th Bde: (less D/105)	S.1.b.0.1. to S.2.a.0.1. also 1 gun on track X.5.a.4.7. to MARTINPUICH. 1 gun on track and trench S.1.b.6.5. to MARTINPUICH. 1 gun on railway S.2.a.0.2. to MARTINPUICH.			From 11.50 p.m. to 1.20 a.m. All fire will be lifted well behind the Switch line – No fire to be nearer Switch line than 300 yards, as patrols are going out. All ground between this 300 yard limit and MARTINPUICH to be searched.
102nd Bde: (less D/102)	S.2.a.0.1. to S.2.a.6.1. also 1 gun on road from S.2.a.5.3. to MARTINPUICH.			

SEVENTH RELIEF.

From 2ỵ a.m. 12th August to 8 a.m. 12th August.

UNIT	OBJECTIVE	RATE	PROJECTILE	REMARKS.
Same as 5th Relief.	SAME AS 5TH RELIEF.	Same as 6th Relief.	Same as 6th Relief.	3.0 to 5.30 a.m. Barrage of 104th and 175th Bdes: will drop on to Switch --- trench as detailed under 5th Relief. Infantry are being warned. At 3.30 a.m.) Search back as 4.10 a.m.) detailed in 5th 5.20 a.m.) Relief.

EIGHT RELIEF.

From 8 a.m. 12th August to 2 p.m. 12th August.

UNIT	OBJECTIVE	RATE	PROJECTILE	REMARKS.
Same as 6th Relief.	SAME AS 6TH RELIEF.	Same as 5th Relief.	SAME AS 5TH RELIEF.	11 to 12 noon. Barrage of 102nd & 105th Bdes: will drop on to Switch Line as detailed in 5th RELIEF. At 9.30 a.m.) Search back as 10.15 a.m.) detailed in 11.30 a.m.) 5th RELIEF. 12.15 p.m.)

NOTE. Details of NINTH and last RELIEF will be issued later.

SECRET.   45th Infantry Brigade No. 710/G.

15th Division.

HEADQUARTERS,
15th DIVISION.
11 AUG. 1916
Reg. No. 1753

Reference your 100/4.G.a. of the 10th instant. Distribution herewith:-

NO MAN'S LAND.	12 platoons 6/7th R.S.Fusiliers. 12 " 6th Cameron Highrs.
FRONT LINE TRENCH.	4 Platoons 6/7th R.S.Fusiliers. 4 " 6th Cameron Highrs.
New trench dug by 9th Gordons Highrs. from BLACK WATCH ALLEY to YORKSHIRE ALLEY.	8 Platoons 11th A & S. Highrs.
CONTALMAISON VILLA.	1 Platoon. 11th A & S. Highrs.
CONTALMAISON.	7 Platoons. 11th A & S. Highrs. 8 Platoons 13th Royal Scots. including a platoon in each of two strong points.
PEAKE WOOD.	8 Platoons 13th Royal Scots.

Allgood   Brigadier - General.,
11/8/16.   Commanding 45th Infantry Brigade.

Copy No.

15th. Division Operation Order No.73.

Reference :-
Special Operation Map No.1.

Headquarters,
15th. Division.
11th. August 1916.

1. 4th. Australian Division on night 12/13th. August is attacking on the line R.34.a.8.6. - 6.5 - 0.3 - R.33.b.5.5. - 3.2.

2. On the night August 12/13th the 15th. Division will attack the enemy SWITCH LINE from S.1.d.9.9 to Point 47 in X.6.a. (MUNSTER ALLEY).
 The 4th. Australian Division have been asked to assist by forming a defensive flank on the left of the attack.
 Zero time will be communicated later.

3. The 46th. Infantry Brigade will attack on the right, the 45th. Infantry Brigade will attack on the left. Dividing line between Brigades 30 yards E of junction of GLOSTER ALLEY with SWITCH LINE (SWITCH ELBOW).

4. (i). The barrage established at 2 p.m. 10th. August on the German SWITCH LINE will be maintained.
 On the 11th and 12th. instants the Heavy Artillery will bombard certain points in the SWITCH LINE. Between the hours of 10 a.m. and 1 p.m. on those days, 70th. AVENUE, parts of LANCS TRENCH, GLOSTER ALLEY SAP and MUNSTER ALLEY SAP will be evacuated.

(ii). Up to fifteen minutes before zero on the 12/13th. activity on the front of attack will be normal. At fifteen minutes before zero the normal barrage will be brought on to the trenches to be attacked.

(iii). On night of 12/13th. an intense bombardment of the objective by the Left Group Divisional Artillery III Corps will commence at zero hours. The fire will lift at the following times :-

 0.2 ... lift 100 yards.
 0.3 ... lift 50 yards.
 0.5 ... lift 50 yards.
 0.7 ... lift 50 yards.

(iv). Detailed instructions regarding the action of the Left Group Divisional Artillery III Corps and Heavy and Corps Artillery will be issued.

5. (i). At zero hour the assaulting Infantry will be formed ready for attack 150 yards from the enemy trench; they will advance at zero hours and will assault close under the Artillery barrage.

(ii). The position will be consolidated :-
 (a). 46th. Infantry Brigade will double block the German SWITCH LINE to the East, construct two strong points to be occupied by
Lewis

Lewis and machine guns north of the SWITCH, open up the SWITCH LINE and connect it with 70th. AVENUE by two boyaux.

(b). 45th. Infantry Brigade will establish a strong point about X.6.a.3.8 to protect the left and three other strong points to the north east of the portion of the SWITCH LINE captured. These points to be occupied by Lewis and machine guns. The captured line will be connected up with GLOSTER ALLEY and MUNSTER ALLEY, and an intermediate communication trench will be dug.

(iii). Infantry patrols will be pushed out inside the barrage to cover the construction of strong points.

6. Medium and Stokes Mortars and machine guns under the orders of the 46th. Infantry Brigade will cover the right flank of the attack, those of the 45th. Infantry Brigade will cover the left.

7. A contact aeroplane patrol will fly over the objective at 6 a.m. 13th. instant. It will sound a Klaxon horn and the advanced line of Infantry will then display flares at the bottom of the trenches.

8. Infantry will carry 220 rounds S.A.A. per rifle. 50% will carry tools.

9. Two platoons 9th. Gordon Highlanders will be at the disposal of each attacking Brigade to connect the SWITCH LINE with present front line.

10. The 44th. Infantry Brigade will form Divisional Reserve and will on the 12th. move two battalions to PEAK WOOD and SCOTS REDOUBT to replace battalions of the 45th. Infantry Brigade under arrangements to be made between Brigades.

11. Watches will be synchronized at the 46th. Infantry Brigade Headquarters SHELTER WOOD at 12 noon on the 12th. instant. Representatives of Artillery Groups and Infantry Brigades to be present.

H. Knox
Lieut. Colonel.
General Staff, 15th. Division.

Issued at 1 a.m.
to :-
```
III Corps.              copies Nos.1 & 2.   A.D.M.S.         Copy No. 11.
III Corps H.Arty.       Copy No.    3.      A.P.M.             ..    12.
34th. Division.             ..      4.      "A" & "Q".         ..    13.
4th. Australian Div.        ..      5.      15th. Div.Arty..   ..    14.
44th. Inf. Bde.             ..      6.      C.R.E.             ..    15.
45th. Inf. Bde.             ..      7.      23rd.Div.Arty...   ..    16.
46th. Inf. Bde.             ..      8.      War Diary.         ..    17.
9th. Gordons.               ..      9.      File.              ..    18.
15th. Signals.              ..     10.
```

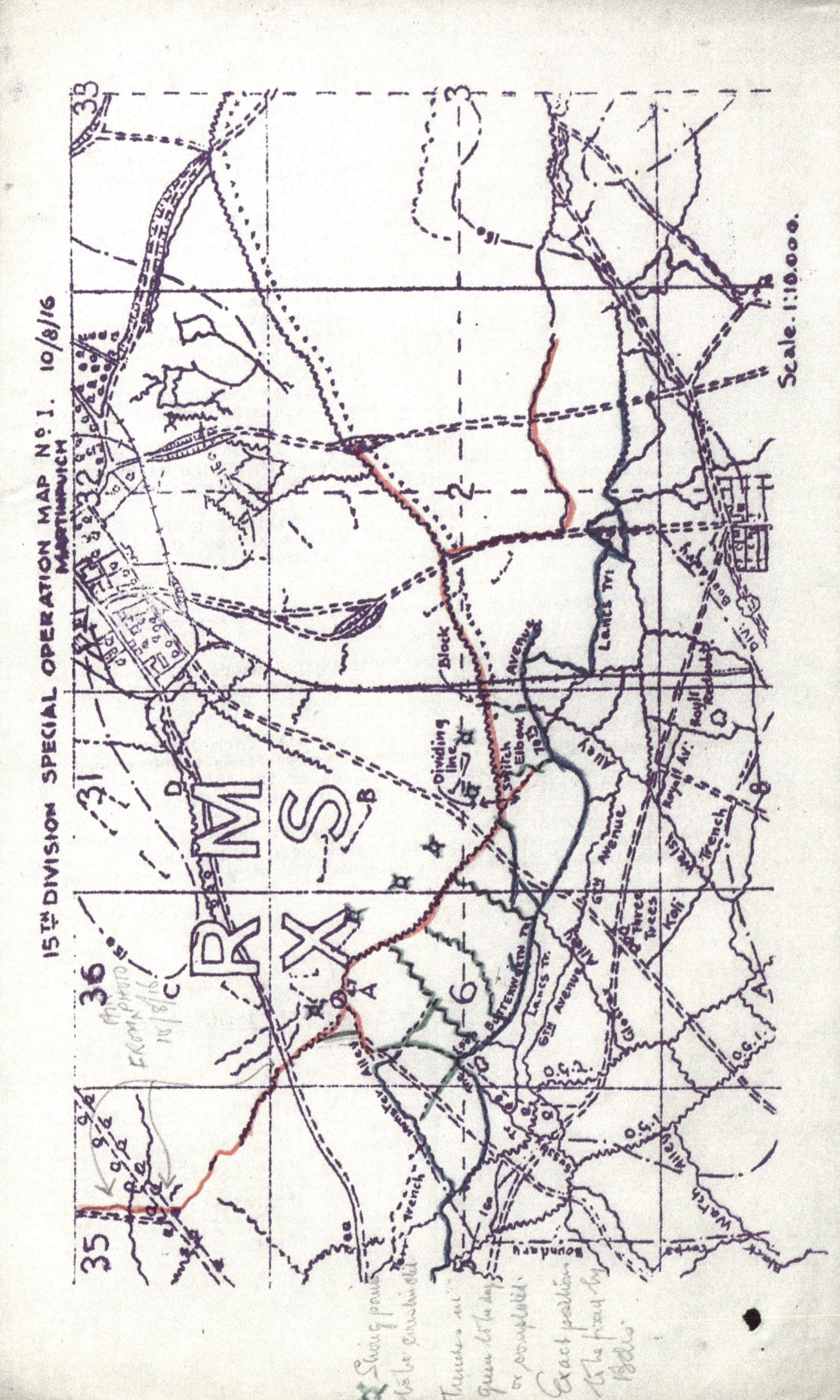

S E C R E T.
COPY NO. 6

III CORPS OPERATION ORDER NO. 108.

Reference:- 10.8.16.
1/10,000 Trench Map.
1/5,000 Operations Trench Map.

1. The 4th Australian Division is, on the night of the 12/13th August, attacking on the line:-

   R.34.a.86. - 65 - 05 - R.35.b.55 - 52.

2. The 15th Division will attack the SWITCH LINE from about S.1.d.99. to the Junction of MUNSTER ALLEY on the night of the 12/13th.

   Zero time will be communicated later.

3. Blocks will be established on the SWITCH LINE at S.1.d.99 and X.6.a.3.8. and strong posts established in front of the line.

4. The 4th Australian Division are being asked to form a defensive flank from the junction of MUNSTER ALLEY with the SWITCH LINE to O.G.2 near THE WINDMILL.

5. On the 11th and 12th, between 10 a.m. and 1 p.m., the Heavy Artillery will bombard the hostile trenches on either side of the SWITCH ELBOW and the 15th Division will arrange to withdraw the infantry from the advanced posts in GLOSTER ALLEY and 70th Avenue during this bombardment.
   Previous to ZERO, the artillery will destroy the SWITCH LINE between MUNSTER ALLEY and the POZIERES - MARTINPUICH Railway.
   On the 11th and 12th, the artillery will also carry out a bombardment of :-

   (i) The remainder of the SWITCH LINE.
   (ii) The trenches round MARTINPUICH.
   (iii) The trench running from the North West Corner of HIGH WOOD through S.3.central.

6. There will be an intensive bombardment of the objective from 0 till 0.2, at which time the barrage will lift 100 yards back from the SWITCH LINE and the infantry will assault.
   At 0.3 the artillery will gradually rake back until at 0.7 it is 250 yards back from the SWITCH LINE.
   Detailed instructions regarding the artillery programme will be issued by the B.G.,R.A., 3rd Corps.

7. A contact aeroplane patrol will fly over the objective at 6 a.m. 13th instant. When this aeroplane is over the infantry it will sound a Klaxon Horn and the advanced line of infantry will display flares at the bottom of the trenches.

8. The 15th Division will be responsible for distributing time to its own brigades and the III Corps Heavy Artillery.

9. Acknowledge on attached slip.

Issued by S.D.R. at 6.50 p.m.

As per standard list.

Brigadier-General,
General Staff
III CORPS.

Headquarters,
    15th Division.

**HEADQUARTERS,
15th DIVISION.**

10 AUG. 1916

No. 1748

Reference 15th Division No 100/4/G.a.
The only alteration in my disposition
on the night of the 12th inst., so far as
my present intentions are, will be that
two companies of my Reserve Battalion will
move up to front area.

                        T. J. Mather

Brigade H.Q.   Brig. Gen.
  August, 1916.   Commanding,
                         46th Inf. Bde

SECRET.

15th Division No. 100 (3)/4 G.s.

44th Inf. Bde.
45th Inf. Bde.
46th Inf. Bde.
9th Gordons.
C.R.E.
23rd Divl. Arty.

Reference para. (iii).(b). of 15th Division No. 100/(2)/4 G.s. of this date.

During following hours it is proposed to drop barrage onto Switch Trench itself between points S.1.b.0.1. and S.2.a.6.1. Infantry should be warned of these hours:-

11th August.

        2   - 2.30 p.m.
        7.45 -   8 p.m.

12th August.

        1.45 - 2 a.m.
        6   - 6.30 a.m.
        11 - 12 noon.
        5.30 - 6 p.m.

2.   If any of these periods are unsuitable or not desired please intimate by wire.

                                                    Lieut. Colonel,

10th August, 1916.   General Staff, 15th Division.

SECRET.

15th Division No. 100 (2)/4 G.a.

44th Inf. Bde.
45th Inf. Bde.
46th Inf. Bde.
9th Gordons.
C.R.E.
23rd Divl. Arty.

---

1. As a result of the conference this afternoon and of a further conference held at the Corps Headquarters, the G.O.C. has decided that the operation against the German Line Switch is to be conducted as below. The Corps Operation Order has not yet been received but the details given may be taken as correct and in the absence of further orders are to be acted on.

(i). The German Line Switch will be bombarded by the Heavy Artillery from 10 a.m. to 1 p.m. on the 11th and 12th insts. 70th AVENUE, part of LANCS TRENCH, GLOSTER ALLEY SAP and MUNSTER ALLEY to be evacuated during these hours.

(ii). To enable our patrols to reconnoitre the German Switch the normal barrage maintained on that line will lift -
on night 10th/11th between 11 p.m. and 12.30 a.m.
on night 11th/12th between 11.50 p.m. and 1.20 a.m.

(iii)(a). On night of 12th, 15 minutes before zero hour the normal barrage will be brought <u>on to</u> the German Switch Line.

(b). This will be practised several times before the 12th to drill the enemy to it. Times will be notified as it will be necessary to clear saps.

(iv) On night of 12th at zero hour (which will be fixed by the Corps) an intense bombardment will start on the enemy's front line and infantry will commence to move forward.

At 0.2 the barrage will lift 100 yards.
 „ 0.3 „   „   „   „   50   „
 „ 0.5 „   „   „   „   50   „
 „ 0.7 „   „   „   „   50   „

NOTE. The reason the G.O.C. has decided on this change is that it is essential that the enemy is not given time to bring his barrage to bear on our men waiting to assault. The sooner they get forward when the intense barrage opens the better. Troops will form up under the normal barrage as in 3 (a).

3. (v). Each Brigade will have a ½ company of the 9th Gordons attached to it to be employed on connecting up the Switch Line with present front line.

(vi). Objectives, etc., etc., as arranged this afternoon.

2. The Division on our left will be engaged in another operation that night but the Corps are asking them to form a defensive flank from MUNSTER ALLEY to the BAUPAUME ROAD. The latest photo shows that the enemy has dug a trench from near X.6.a.4.7. across railway to road in R.35.d. central.

3. Operation Orders will be issued as soon as possible.

4. ACKNOWLEDGE.

Lieut. Colonel,
General Staff, 15th Division.

10th Aug., 1916.

SECRET.

COPY NO: 1

S/1/83.   R.A. 23rd Division Order No: 56.

Reference:- Sketch issued.   10th August, 1916.

1.   With a view to subsequent attack, that portion of the German Switch Line which lies between about S.1.d.9½.9. and X.6.a.4.7. will be isolated as far as possible by Artillery fire day and night from now onwards.   This fire will be continuous in order to prevent reliefs, and supply of water, food, ammunition, etc, to the Garrison.

2.   Artillery programme is attached.

3.   Watches will be checked with R.A. H.Q. at 12 noon and 11 p.m. daily.

4.   ACKNOWLEDGE.

A. K. Hay.
Major,

Issued at   Brigade Major R.A. 23rd Division.

Copies No: 1 to 4   15th Division.
           5   R.A. IIIrd Corps.
           6   Lahore Artillery.
           7   34th Div: Artillery.
           8   1st Div: Artillery.
        9 to 13   102nd Bde: R.F.A.
       14 to 18   103rd   "   "
       19 to 23   104th   "   "
       24 to 28   105th   "   "
       29 to 32   175th   "   "
       34 to 38   25th   "   "
       39 & 40   Diary.

Copy N° 2 To 44 Bd
     "   3   45   "
         4   46   "

FIRST RELIEF.

From 2 p.m. 10th August to 8 p.m. 10th August.

UNIT	OBJECTIVES	RATE	PROJECTILE	REMARKS.
L/325	Block Switch Trench at about S.2.a.6.2.	1 Round per gun per 5 minutes.	H. E.	Each Battery will at once fire an observed series of 100 rounds to establish a block — subsequently continuing at 1 round per gun per 5 minutes.
D/105	Block Switch Trench at X.6.a.4.7.			
103rd Bde:	Switch Line X.3.a.4.7. to S.1.b.0.1.	1 Round per gun per 5 minutes.	5 Shrapnel to 1 H.E.	At 3.10 p.m.) Search slowly 4.15 p.m.) back behind 5.35 p.m.) Switch Line in 6.20 p.m.) 50 yard searches 7.45 p.m.) to MARTINPUICH,) returning again) suddenly to) original barrage
104th Bde:	S.1.b.0.1. to S.2.a.0.1. also 1 gun on track X.6.a.4.7. to MARTINPUICH. 1 gun on track and trench S.1.b.3.6. to MARTINPUICH. 1 gun on railway S.2.a.0.2. to MARTINPUICH.			
175th Bde:	S.2.a.0.1. to S.2.a.6.1. also 1 gun on road S.2.a.5.6. to MARTINPUICH.			

SECOND RELIEF.
From 8 p.m. 10th August to 2 a.m. 11th August.

UNIT	OBJECTIVE	RATE	PROJECTILE	REMARKS.
D/102	Switch Trench at about S.2.a.6.2.	1 Round per gun per 3 minutes.	H. E.	Exact points must be ascertained by Battery Commanders from O.C. D/25 and D/103 and registered in daylight.
D/104	Switch Trench at X.6.a.4.7.			
1 Section 46th Bty:	Enfilade Switch Trench from S.1.b.0.1. to X.6.a.4.7.	1 Round per gun per 2 minutes.	5 Shrapnel to 1 H. E.	At 8.50 p.m. Lift suddenly 500 yards back, and search slowly back to original barrage dropping 50 yards at a time.
25th Bde:	Switch Trench from S.1.b.0.1. to X.6.a.4.7.			9.40 p.m.
105th Bde:	S.1.b.0.1. to S.2.a.6.1. also 1 gun on track X.6.a.4.7. to MARTINPUICH. 1 gun on track and trench S.1.b.6.6. to MARTINPUICH. 1 gun on railway S.2.a.0.2. to MARTINPUICH.			10.55 p.m. 12 midnight 1.20 a.m.
102nd Bde:	S.2.a.0.1. to S.2.a.6.1. also 1 gun on road S.2.a.5.6. to MARTINPUICH			

SUBSEQUENT RELIEFS.

THIRD RELIEF. From 2 a.m. to 8 a.m. 11th August. Details as for 1st RELIEF except rate of fire to be as for 2nd RELIEF. Hours for lifts will be 2.30, 4.10 5.40, 6.50 a.m.

FOURTH RELIEF. From 8 a.m. to 2 p.m. 11th August. Details as for 2nd RELIEF, except rate of fire to be as for 1st RELIEF. Hours for lifts to be as for 2nd RELIEF.

FURTHER RELIEFS WILL BE NOTIFIED LATER.

Draft
Discussed at Conference

DRAFT.

15th.(Scottish) Division.

Preliminary Operation Order.

Ref:-
Special Operation Map No.1.

10/8/16

1. In conjunction with a larger operation, the Division will, on August 12th., occupy the German SWITCH LINE from 80 yards west of Railway in S.2.c. to Point 47 in X.6.a. (MUNSTER ALLEY).

2. (i). The 46th. Infantry Brigade will attack on the right; the 45th. Infantry Brigade will attack on the left.
   (ii). The dividing point in the objective 20 yards east of Point 38.
   (iii). The Artillery programme and zero hour will be communicated later.
   (iv). The leading wave of the attack of both Brigades is to move in close to the Artillery barrage.

3. The position will be consolidated :-
   (i). 46th. Infantry Brigade will double block the German SWITCH LINE to the East, construct two strong points to be occupied by Lewis and Machine Guns North of the SWITCH, open up the SWITCH LINE and connect it with 70th. AVENUE by two boyaux.

   (ii). The 45th. Inf. Bde. will establish a strong point about X.6.a.3.8 to protect the left and three other strong points to the N.E. of the portion of the SWITCH LINE captured. These points to be occupied by Lewis and Machine guns. The captured line will be connected up with GLOSTER ALLEY and MUNSTER ALLEY, the intermediate saps now being constructed being jumped forward as opportunity offers.

4. Stokes mortars and machine guns under the orders of the 46th. Inf. Bde will cover the right flank of the attack, those of the 45th. Inf. Bde. will cover the left flank.

5. Infantry will carry 220 rounds S.A.A. per rifle; 50% of leading waves will carry tools.

6. Infantry patrols will be pushed out inside our barrage to cover the construction of strong points.

7. The 44th. Infantry Bde. will be disposed as follows by   a.m.

Officers of the 44th. Inf. Bde. will be present at Brigade Hd. Qrs. of 45th. and 46th. Inf. Bdes to keep in touch with the situation.
The Brigade will not move forward from the above area without orders from the Division.

8. Watches will be checked at 9 a.m. and 12 noon 12th. instant with General Staff, 15th. Division.

at HQ 46th Inf Bde

"C" Form (Duplicate).
MESSAGES AND SIGNALS.

Service Instructions. Priority

Handed in at .... Office .... m. Received .... m.

TO   Arty 23rd Div

Sender's Number	Day of Month	In reply to Number	AAA
AA 770	10		

[message body illegible in pencil]

FROM ....
PLACE & TIME .... 9.45 a.m.

15th Division.No.100/4 G.a.

45th Inf. Bde.
46th Inf. Bde.

Please report as early as possible how you will have your Battalions disposed at Zero hour on 12th. The G.O.C. wishes to have this information to enable him to order the disposal of the Reserve Brigade some of the Battalions of which will replace your Reserve Battalions but will be under Divisional orders.

(sd) *[signature]*

Lieut. Colonel,

10th August, 1916.   General Staff, 15th Division.

Verbal:—
46th Bde — 2 Coys of Reserve *[forward]*

45th Bde
Peak Wood
& Scots Redoubt — empty.
[initials] 10/8/16

15th Division No. 100/4 G.s.

45th Inf. Bde.
46th Inf. Bde.
23rd D. Artillery.

1. The German Switch Line between S.2.a.0.0. and X.6.a.2.9. will be isolated by fire until further order to prevent food, etc., etc., reaching the garrison.
Fire to be continuous by day and night except over places that can be clearly seen.

2. The artillery are arranging to do this, commencing at 2 p.m. to-day. It will not be necessary to vacate any of our trenches.

3. Brigades will arrange to supplement this artillery fire by direct and indirect machine gun fire.

Lieut. Colonel,
10th Aug., 1916. General Staff, 15th Division.

SECRET

HEADQUARTERS,
15th DIVISION.
9 AUG.1916
Reg. No. 1215

Copy No 12

Preliminary Operation Order.

9.8.16.

1. Warning has been received that the 15th Division is to be prepared to capture the GERMAN SWITCH LINE on the line BAC. 45th Infantry Brigade being responsible from B. to A. and 46th Inf.Bde. from A. to C.
The point A will be 30 yds east of the salient in the German Switch Line at S.1.d.3½.8. . The point C. will be about 80 yds west of the Railway which crosses the German Switch Line at S.2.a.0.0.

The point B is 750 yds NW of A.

2. This operation will be carried out on the afternoon of the 11th inst.

3. The 12th High.L.I. will carry out this operation on the front A - C and will take over temporarily on the 11th inst. such portion of 70th AVENUE as is required . The point C. will be about 80 yds West of the railway crossing the GERMAN SWITCH LINE.

4. The following work is to be begun at once and pushed on with all possible speed day and night.

(a) Under arrangements to be made by O.C.
7th/8th K.O.Sco.Bord.

(i) To open up the continuation of WELCH ALLEY for 50 yds i.e. to point K. on plan, thence the trench will take a new line as shown in plan to L. This deviation is also to be dug as far as possible . This cancells instructions given to Major Hart this morning.

(ii) The preparation and facilities for getting over the parapet in 70th AVENUE, after consultation with O.C., 12th High.L.I.

(b) Under arrangements to be made by O.C., 12th High.L.I.

(i) To begin digging a trench from a point W. to as shown in attached plan. The point W. being about 50 yds mark WEST of X.

(ii) To make the ground so that the attack can get a fair start on a line parallel to the objective as shown by the dotted line T.D. on plan. This might either be dug or taped, it may not be necessary to mark the whole length or it might be marked on lines in echelon to each other . It might even not be necessary to mark any portion of the line except West of the point W.

5. The orders for attack will direct O.C., 12th High.L.I. to attack with three companies in the Front Line. The first wave will consist of 6 platoons, two platoons in each company . The second wave will be formed similarly. The third wave will consist of one company in line,

2.

6. Tools will be carried by at least 50% of the first two waves. Arrangements must be made to take sandbags across for blocking the trench on the right.

7. Two blocks are to be made on the Right. One at point C., the other at point Z., 40 yds apart.

8. The 10th Sco.Rif. will relieve 7/8th K.O.Sco.Bord. on the 10th inst. and 10/11th High.L.I. will relieve 12th High.L.I. on the 12th inst.

9. 46th Trench Mortar Battery will be prepared to operate on the GERMAN SWITCH LINE from the Railway eastwards and along that portion of the INTERMEDIATE LINE running South from the German Switch Line.
Medium Trench Mortar Battery will do likewise.

10. O.C., 46th Machine Gun Company will arrange for enemy's trenches East of the point C., including the Intermediate Line to be swept by Machine Gun fire during the attack.

Captain,
Bde Maj.,
46th Inf. Bde.

Issued at
through Signals.

Copy No 1. File
2. War Diary
3. 7/8th K.O.Sco.Bord.
4. 10th Sco.Rif.
5. 10/11th High.L.I.
6. 12th High.L.I.
7. 46th M.G. Company
8. 46th Trench Mortar Battery
9. Medium Trench M. Bty
10. 73rd R.E. Coy.
11. 45th Inf.Bde.
12. 15th Division.

Plan to accompany Preliminary Operation Order dated 9-8-16

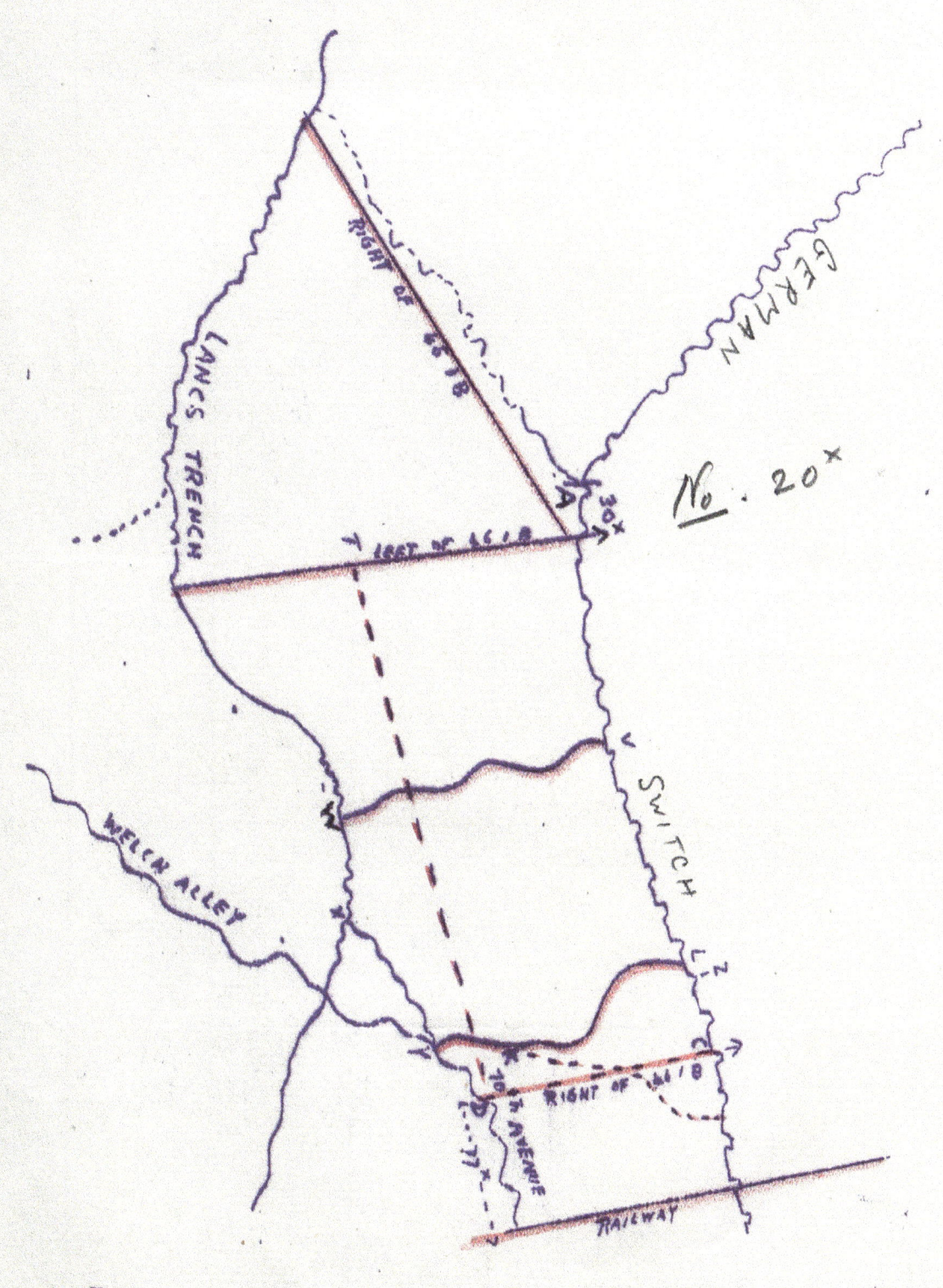

Note

Goss saw B.G.C. 45th Bde in Contalmaison & discussed the attack 6 a.m. 9/8/16

I saw both 45th & 46th Inf Bdes Commdrs together in Shelter Wood at 10 a.m. 9/8/16

Result of these discussions:—

(1) 46th Bde will attack with one battalion left 20x east of ㊳; right — B.G.C. will fix probably about where old trench from 70th Avenue to Switch meets Switch. He will double block switch & will cover block with Stokes from 70th Avenue.

(2) 45th Bde will attack with two battalions. Rifle Bde will take advantage of cover provided by ground & thistles. Trenches will be dug to shelter left Bte. German trenches about ㊼ to be well dow in. Sap are being dug out from Butterworth trench.

B.G. 45th Inf Bde wants to know exactly what Australian situation is.

Genl Matthews asked if trench towards A could be dug by starting line. I said yes. JHK

(3) 45th Bde will make four strong points in front — 46th Bde will make 2 strong points.

(4) Both Bdes want Stokes.

(5) Artillery must deal with High Wood & shell holes beyond Switch

JHK
9/8/16

Headquarters,
    15th Division.

**HEADQUARTERS,
15th DIVISION.
9- AUG.1916
Reg. No. 1702**

Reference 100/4/G.a. dated 7th inst. paras 3 and 4.

1. I think it will be exceedingly difficult to dig the trench shown by black dotted line on the sketch, to G.38 unless the line AC is taken at the same time in fact it would be practically impossible unless it was sapped.

2. Unless the whole of that portion of the Intermediate Trench, not captured by the 11th inst. is heavily barraged, it will be difficult to take the line A.C., but if this trench (if any exists on that date) is heavily barraged and the portion of the German Switch further to the east. I think it would be possible to take the line A.C. as proposed by the Divisional Commander.

3. The connecting of C. and D. will, in my opinion, be practically impossible if dug on top, so long as Germans are in the Switch line East of C, it could, however, be sapped and both communications D and the one connecting point 38 might be begun at once by sapping, but this would probably show the enemy what was intended.

4. There is an extension of WELCH ALLEY beyond our Front Line which might be improved and thus facilitate a communication trench being constructed in that locality in place of the one actually sited as ~~sighted another or the one A.C.~~ sited as DC.

Brigade Headquarters,
    9ᵗʰ August, 1916.

                                Brig.Gen.
                                Commanding,
                                46th INF.BDE

SECRET.

15th. Div.
No.100/4 G.a.

44th. Inf. Bde.   C.R.E.
45th. Inf. Bde.   9th. Gordons.
46th. Inf. Bde.

---

1. Warning has been received that the Division is to be prepared to capture the GERMAN SWITCH LINE between points A and B possibly on the afternoon of the 11th. August. This operation, if ordered, will be carried out by the 45th. Infantry Brigade.

2. On attached sketch the existing front line is shown in red. The work ordered by the Corps to be carried out on the night 7/8th is shown in blue. The work required in preparation for the attack is indicated in green.

3. To assist the 45th. Infantry Brigade on the 11th. August, the 46th. Infantry Brigade will be prepared to bring heavy Stokes Mortar fire on the GERMAN SWITCH east of A; further when the 45th. Infantry Brigade have established a block at A the 46th. Infantry Brigade will dig a trench as shown by black dotted line to connect with Point 38.

4. It appears to the Divisional Commander that it might help the 45th. Infantry Brigade if the 46th. Infantry Brigade were to carry out a simultaneous attack on the SWITCH LINE between Point (c) and 38, blocking the SWITCH to the east and connecting (c) and (d). This is only a proposal additional to the operation for which we have been warned to prepare; so far it has not the approval of the Corps. The Divisional Commander would be glad of the opinion of the Brigadier General Commanding 46th. Infantry Brigade.

5. The 9th. Gordon Highlanders will place one company at the disposal of the 45th. Infantry Brigade to dig a trench approximately as shown in green and red in X.11. The Officer Commanding Company to report to the Brigadier General Commanding 45th. Infantry Brigade at Brigade Headquarters, CONTALMAISON by 5 p.m. tomorrow.

6. ACKNOWLEDGE.

7th. August 1916.   Lieut. Colonel.
General Staff, 15th. Division.

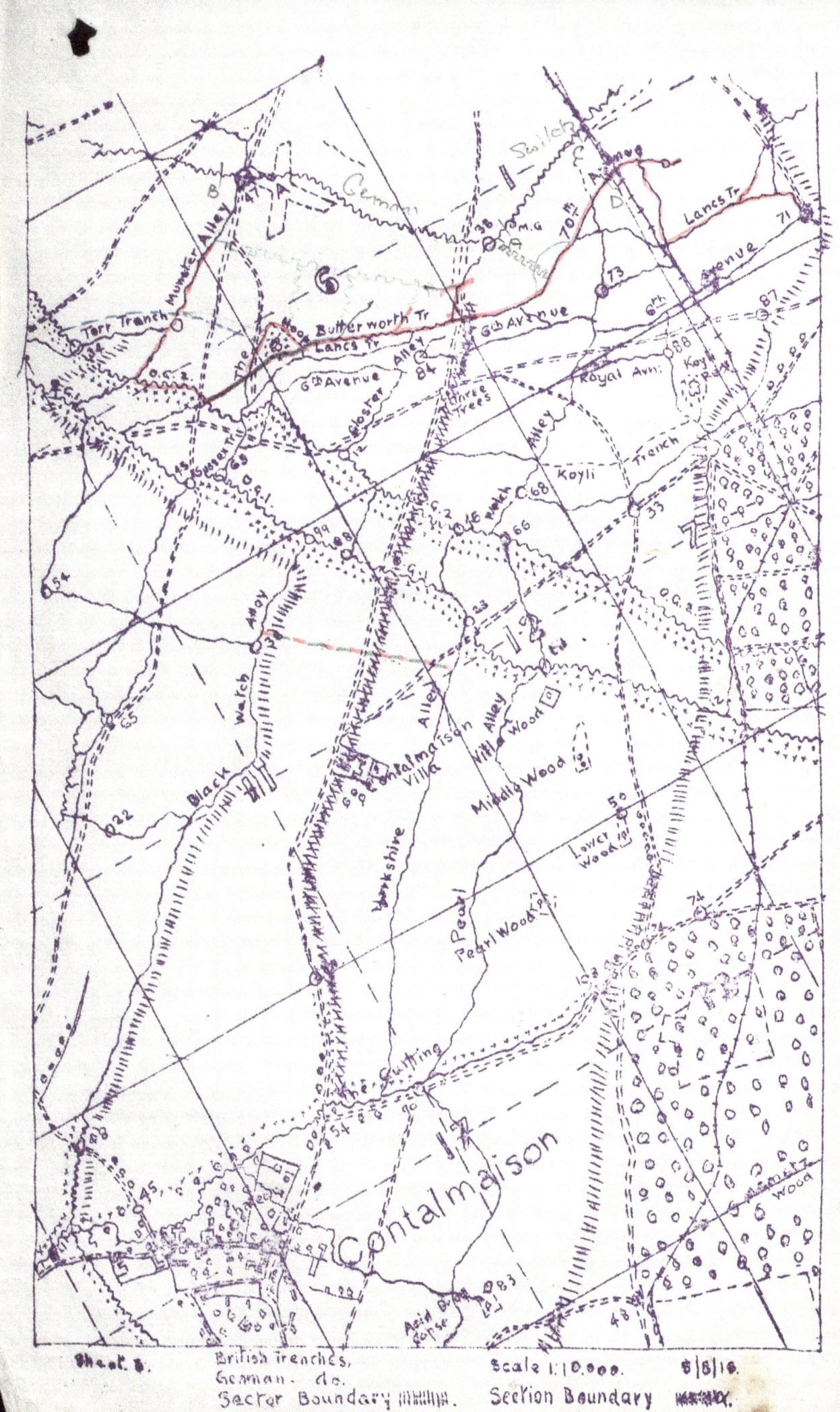

W. 15517—M. 141. 250,000. 1/16. L.S.&Co. Forms/W 3091/2.   Army Form W. 3091.

Cover for Documents.

Keep-

100/8

Nature of Enclosures.

OPERATIONS. -against INTERMEDIATE LINE-by 15th. Div.

Notes, or Letters written.

SECRET.

15th Div. No. 100/8 G.a.

45th Inf. Bde.
_____

1. A tracing from photos taken yesterday, 31st August, is forwarded.

2. The main points brought out are :-

(a). There is no sign of German work our side of BOTTOM TRENCH WEST.

(b). There are distinct signs of an attempt to dig a trench southward from the middle of BOTTOM TRENCH EAST. This work should be carefully patrolled.

(c). The late German trench ending at S.2.c.9.9. and our trench (MACFARLANE ALLEY) running south along east side of road from S.2.a.7.2. are heading for each other and offer the best route for joining up.

SWANSEA TRENCH west of road in S.2.b. has been traced too straight and the attempt to get a continuous trench at once has resulted in the dissipation of effort. This morning's reports of the trench show it to be very shallow and practically indefensible for the 100 - 150 yards nearest the road.
The G.O.C. directs that work be concentrated, as originally ordered on several properly traced traversed posts to be completed to full depth before any further work is done on the continuous trench.

K. Henderson Major
for Lieut. Colonel,
1.9.16. General Staff, 15th Division.

SECRET.

15th Division No. 100/8 G.a.

(Spare)

45th Inf. Bde.
46th Inf. Bde.
C.R.E.
Left Group D.A.

---

1.   A tracing from photos taken yesterday, 31st August, is forwarded.

2.   The main points brought out are :-

(a).   There is no sign of German work our side of BOTTOM TRENCH WEST.

(b).   There are distinct signs of an attempt to dig a trench southward from the middle of BOTTOM TRENCH EAST. This work should be carefully patrolled.

(c).   The late German trench ending at S.2.c.9.9. and our trench (MACFARLANE ALLEY) running south along east side of road from S.2.a.7.2. are heading for each other and offer the best route for joining up.

Lieut. Colonel,

1.9.16.   General Staff, 15th Division.

SKETCH FROM AIR PHOTOS.
1/9/16.   1:5,000.

A — Bottom Road
S
B
C — Pioneer Alley, Fusilier Alley, Lane's ?, Intermediate Trench
D — Somme Alley, Jutland Alley, 6th Avenue East, Cardiff Trench

To,
46th Infantry Brigade

REPORT OF PATROL THAT RECONNOITRED INTERMEDIATE LINE 30/8/16.

Between 5 p.m. and 6 p.m. a considerable number of the enemy were seen giving themselves up to the 45th Brigade and others who attempted instead to escape in the direction of the SWITCH LINE were heavily fired on from the left strong point. At 6 p.m. 2nd Lt. R.J. Burns, O.C. B Company sent 2nd Lt. S.H. Barnet with a corporal and two men to find out if the INTERMEDIATE TRENCH was cleared and establish connection with the 45th Bde.

The patrol crossed our block and advanced along the parados to the ELBOW where they found a party of 4 officers 2 N.C.Os and 13 men. With the exception of 1 officer all these belonged to the 17th Regt. One officer belonged to the 23rd Bay Regt. 2nd Lieut. Barnet sent these prisoners, who came without opposition, back under escort and went again with the same party to get in touch with the 45th Bde. He succeeded in establishing connection with the Royal Scots Fusiliers but was wounded in the wrist while making his way over the trench near the ELBOW and the Corporal with him was badly wounded. A block was temporarily established at the ELBOW and during the night the trench was cleared and connected up to this point. The patrol reports that the centre portion of this trench was reasonably good and the rest badly broken up. 2nd Lt. Barnett estimates the number of dead in the trench at least 50. There were no wounded in the part held by us. The dead belonged to various Regiments, 100, 101, 133, 179, 181 and those belonging to the first 3 regiments had been much longer dead than those of the last two. The dead of the 179th and 181st were found in the westernmost end of the trench. The trench contained a large quantity of S.A.A. and bombs and 2 Machine Guns were taken, one without a lock and lying on the parados, the other in a shell hole fitted with belt and apparently ready for action.

(Sgd) R. NASMITH, Captain
& Adjt. for
Lt. Col.
Commanding,
10/11th High.L.I.

SECRET.

15th. Div.
No.100(2)/8 G.a.

45th. Inf. Bde.
46th. Inf. Bde.
Left Group D.A.
C.R.E.
9th. Gordons.
----

1. The following is to be the policy and order inportance of work resulting from the capture of the INTERMEDIATE TRENCH :-

(b). ~~(a).~~ Join up SANDERSON TRENCH with north end of INTERMEDIATE LINE at S.2.c.9.9.

(c). ~~(b).~~ Connect LANCS SAP with INTERMEDIATE LINE ELBOW and consolidate INTERMEDIATE LINE as support line to SWANSEA TRENCH.

(a). ~~(c).~~ Complete SWANSEA TRENCH, and where field of fire from it is unsatisfactory establish posts in front of it.

2. The G.O.C. again wishes to impress on Infantry and Artillery the importance of preparing for counter-attack and of stocking posts with all requisites.

3. He also hopes a lookout will be kept for catching parties of the enemy making for the INTERMEDIATE LINE in ignorance of its capture.

30th. August 1916.

K Henderson
Major,
General Staff, 15th Division.

"C" Form (Duplicate).   Army Form C. 2123.
MESSAGES AND SIGNALS.

Service Instructions. Priority

Handed in at........... Office ...... m. Received 6 55 m.

TO 15th Div

Sender's Number	Day of Month	In reply to Number	AAA
7 164	30 Aug		

As soon as the INTERMEDIATE LINE has been cleared tonight the Corps Commander wishes you to join up SANDERSON Trench to north end of INTERMEDIATE line at S.2.C.9.9 — Dig a new trench across the corner of the INTERMEDIATE LINE from S.2.D.0.1 to S.2.D.3.5 and use this line as a support line to SWANSEA trench aaa To join up posts in line of SWANSEA trench and throw out a line of posts with a good field of fire in front of this line aaa also to

FROM
PLACE & TIME

"C" Form (Duplicate).
MESSAGES AND SIGNALS.

Army Form C.2123.

	3yd 123	Charges to Pay. £ s.	Office Stamp.
Service Instructions.			
Handed in at ..... Office ..6.. m. Received 6.5 p.m.			
TO	15th Div		

Sender's Number	Day of Month	In reply to Number	A A A
G764	30		

Take every precaution possible to meet expected counter attack in S 2.B tonight and for all arrangements for catching parties of the enemy bringing up stores to the INTERMEDIATE LINE

6.58

FROM PLACE & TIME	3rd Corps 6.30 pm

"A" Form.   Army Form C. 2121.
MESSAGES AND SIGNALS.

TO: 15th DIV

Sender's Number: BM 979
Day of Month: 30th
AAA

Preliminary Report on progress of Work on Swansea Trench

1. An officer of 74" Fd Coy RE laid out the tape & marked out the position of four strong points.

2. In endeavouring to get touch with the 45th Bde this officer followed a couple of men whom he saw get into a trench. He went up to the trench & began talking, but immediately found that the men in the trench were talking German. There were 5 to 10 of the enemy there. He emptied his revolver

"A" Form. Army Form C. 2121.
MESSAGES AND SIGNALS.

Prefix......Code......m.	Words	Charge	This message is on a/c of:	Recd. at......m.
Office of Origin and Service Instructions.	Sent		..............Service.	Date..............
....	At.........m.			From............
....	To............			
....	By............		(Signature of "Franking Officer.")	By............

TO {

Sender's Number	Day of Month	In reply to Number	
			AAA

into them and got away.
This trench is estimated to be
at S.2.d.2.8.

3. Four Strong Points were
commenced and carried
on until dawn.

4. Two of these strong points
were completed to a depth
of about 4½ feet and are
held. The position of these
are approximately S 2 d 7 to 10.
and S 2 d 5 9

5. The other two are not
so far advanced.

From 46th IB
Place
Time 10.50 a

Signature: [signed] Capt.
m. GOC 46 IB

S E C R E T.

15th Division No. 100(1)/8 G.a.

45th Inf. Bde.
46th Inf. Bde.
9th Gordons.
C.R.E.

Reference attached report and sketch.

1. The G.O.C. draws attention to Lieut. SANDERSON'S reconnaissance. This shows the siting of the posts to be irregular and the intervals excessive except in one case.

2. He attaches the greatest importance to the completion of the chain at 40 yards intervals tonight, and its eventual completion to a continuous trench.

3. Attention is drawn to the names allotted to the two new communication trenches dug by 9th Gordons. These also must be pushed on with all possible speed.

4. The siting of some posts gives very bad view and field of fire, the line having gone somewhat low in the dip. The new posts to be interpolated should be put more forward as far as possible, and their site should be reconnoitred and fixed by day.

K Henderson Major
for
Lieut. Colonel,
General Staff, 15th Division.

30th Aug., 1916.

SECRET.

15th Division No. 100/9 G.a.

III Corps.
——————————

The following is the situation as far as ascertainable in
S.2.d. :-

Five posts have been put out, two by 45th Inf. Bde. west
of road, three by 46th Inf. Bde. east of road. 45th Inf. Bde.
right is 120 yards from 46th Inf. Bde. left and is continuously
linked to SANDERSON TRENCH. Further posts will be put in gaps
tonight. The two Brigades are in touch, officers have been
across to each other, and flank posts are in view of each other.
46th Inf. Bde. hold small length of trench at S.2.d.6.8. Some
Germans tried to pass during night but not ascertainable in which
direction. There was some fighting, several Germans were killed,
and one man 17th Bavarian Infantry Regiment captured by 45th Inf.
Bde. The Germans are still in the INTERMEDIATE LINE. An R.E.
officer approached them by mistake and fired his revolver at them,
and they put up Very Lights.

Sap ending S.2.d.4.4. was extended along east of road to
INTERMEDIATE TRENCH, but shallow. Communication trench dug from
S.2.d.9.2. due north 3 feet deep as far as INTERMEDIATE TRENCH,
beyond that to within 115 yards of present extremity (about
S.2.b.3.0.) of CLARKE'S TRENCH extension, to average depth of
4½ feet.

Attached sketch shows route and report of Lieut. SANDERSON
Duke of Lancaster's Yeomanry, who has just returned from a
reconnaissance of the situation.

Major General,

30th Aug., 1916.   Commanding, 15th (Scottish) Division.

Copy to :-
       1st Division.   )
       4th Australian Division.)
       Left Group D.A.   )
       G.R.E.   ) For information.
       9th Gordons.   )
       45th Inf. Bde.   )
       46th Inf. Bde.   )

* Count Trenches Knupf.
This should have the effect
1) Taking on the intermediate
  if so consolidation with be
  carried out by joining up
  S20 9-15 to S26.9.0 —
  a special party over nothing
  else but work as tunnel
  point.   fro. Maux on)

in consequence of which I
will take A to B. on
evening of 29/5. Artillery
to keep at it — my S.T.M.
have been ordered to do
the same — zero I suggest
8 p.m. I must have some
pioneers to help to cut

27.VIII.16

Dear Henderson

You not. etc.

[sketch map with labels: SANDERSON TR., BOSCH TR., PIONEER ALLEY, 103°, A, B]

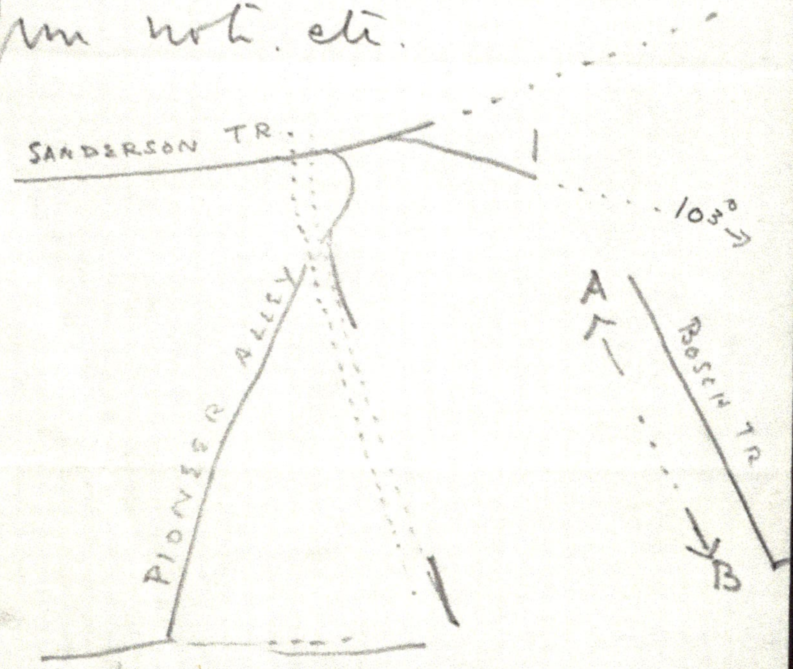

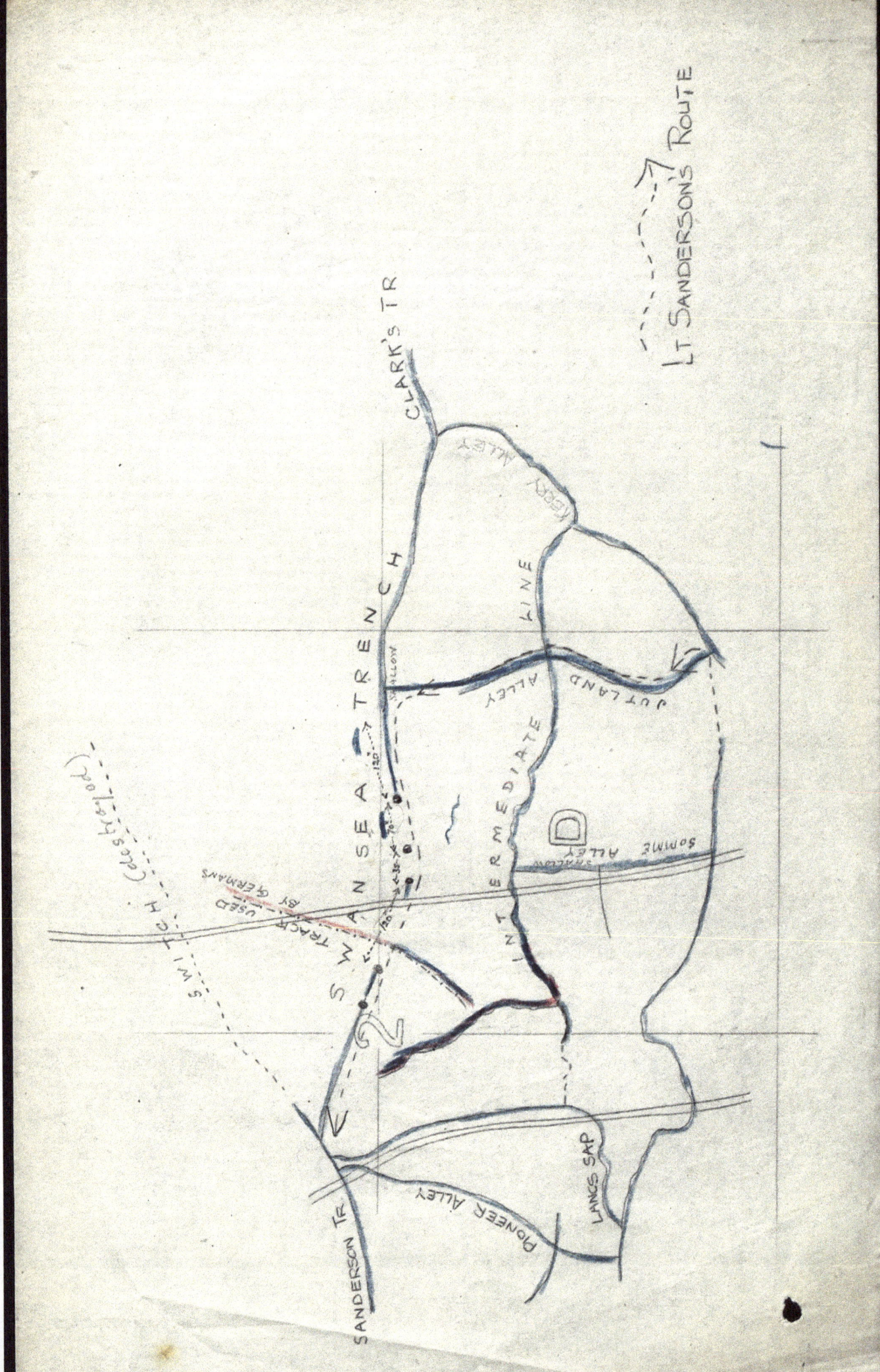

SECRET.

15th Division No. 100/8 G.a.

46th Infantry Brigade.

Reference your B.M./48/16 of 27.8.16.

1. You will remain responsible for the extension of CLARKE'S TRENCH and for the new gains in the INTERMEDIATE LINE as long as access to them is possible from your area only.

2. The plans of the Brigadier General Commanding 45th Infantry Brigade for attacking the INTERMEDIATE LINE include the construction of a communication trench leading to the western end of the part now in your possession, from his present front line south of it. This is being started tonight.

3. The General Officer Commanding intends to make a communication trench from the INTERMEDIATE LINE about S.3.c.0.6. to run north-west to the CLARKE'S TRENCH Extension. This will be dug by the 9th Gordons.

4. When the two trenches referred to in paras. 2 and 3 have been made, or when access has been opened from the west, whichever happens first, the Centre Section Brigade will take over from you the INTERMEDIATE LINE and CLARKE'S TRENCH Extension, west of a line running due north from S.2.d.8.5. (the inter-section limit under 15th Division Operation Order No. 78).

K Henderson Major
for Lieut. Colonel,
General Staff, 15th Division.

27th Aug., 1916.

Copy to :-
45th Inf. Bde.
C.R.E.
} For information.

SECRET.

15th Division No. 100/8 G.a.

46th Infantry Brigade.

Reference your B.M./46/16 of 27.8.16.

1.   You will remain responsible for the extension of CLARKE'S TRENCH and for the new gains in the INTERMEDIATE LINE as long as access to them is possible from your area only.

2.   The plans of the Brigadier General Commanding 45th Infantry Brigade for attacking the INTERMEDIATE LINE include the construction of a communication trench leading to the western end of the part now in your possession, from his present front line south of it.   This is being started tonight.

3.   The General Officer Commanding, also intends to make a communication trench from the INTERMEDIATE LINE about S.3.c.0.6. to run north-west to the CLARKE'S TRENCH Extension.   This will be dug by the 9th Gordons.

4.   When the two trenches referred to in paras. 2 and 3 have been made, or when access has been opened from the west, whichever happens first, the Centre Section Brigade will take over from you the INTERMEDIATE LINE and CLARKE'S TRENCH Extension, west of a line running due north from S.2.d.8.5. (the inter-section limit under 15th Division Operation Order No. 78).

Lieut. Colonel,

27th Aug., 1916.   General Staff, 15th Division.

Copy to :-
          45th Inf. Bde. }
          C.R.E.   } For information.

Headquarters,
15th Division.

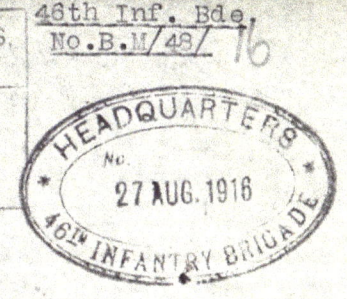

Ref: from 100(I)/P.S.a.

1. As the continuation of CLARKES TRENCH to the N.W. is proceeded with will you please inform me if I will remain responsible for occupying this new trench, my only channel of communication being from S.3.c.5.8., or will 45th Inf. Bde. take over a portion as it is extended across their front.

2. I would like instructions also regarding the INTERMEDIATE LINE which I am now told is occupied by British troops up to a point 200 yards W. of where it was held yesterday morning.
Will the taking of this line rest with me or the 45th Inf. Bde., and is it to be proceeded with ?

and S.2.d.7.2/

3. It seems essential that a Communication Trench be dug from a point between S.2.d.9.2 up to the INTERMEDIATE LINE. Which Brigade is to undertake this ?.

Brigade Headquarters,

27th August, 1916.

Brig. Gen.,

Commanding 46th Inf. Bde.

SECRET.

15th Division No. 100(1)/8 G.a.

46th Infantry Brigade.
....

1. When you have taken over the new frontage from the 1st Division the following will be your policy :-

(a). Continue to prolong CLARKE'S TRENCH (which is reported to have reached approximately S.2.d.9.9.) so as to join it up with the SWITCH LINE about S.2.a.9.2.

(b). Push forward from this line towards the high ground about S.3.a.5.9. in order to obtain a position whence to gain the SWITCH LINE in M.33.c. and d. There is already a post in S.3.b. which should be extended to both flanks as an advanced line to CLARKE'S TRENCH. The 1st Division on your right will be ordered to gain the northern edge of HIGH WOOD and to connect up with your right.

2. It must be impressed on all ranks that the above is important and calls for just as much self sacrifice and devotion as an attack. Work must be carried on in spite of the enemy. At the same time the latter should be harassed by constant artillery and machine gun fire especially at night. Points from which his line can be enfiladed and overlooked should be sought for.

sd. H. Henderson Major

Lieut. Colonel,

26th Aug., 1916.   General Staff, 15th Division.

Copy to :-
    C.R.E.
    C.R.A. Left Group D.A.

SECRET.

15th Division No. 100/8 G.a.

45th Infantry Brigade.
....

1. When you have extended your front the following will be your policy :-

(a). Continue pushing SANDERSON TRENCH eastward to meet the prolongation of CLARKE'S TRENCH.

(b). Continue pushing out strong posts from CAMERON TRENCH to form a line 200 yards from BOTTOM TRENCH.

(c). (i). If the situation in the INTERMEDIATE LINE has not been cleared up by the time you take over, to gain possession of this trench on the 29th inst. and join it up by communication trenches to the prolongations of CLARKE'S and SANDERSON TRENCHES.

(ii). To enable you to make the necessary preparations by the 29th inst., Pioneer assistance will be given you. The C.R.E. will call on you tomorrow to arrange.

(iii). The Heavy Artillery are being asked to make proposals for repeated periodical bombardments of the objective daily till the 29th. On receipt of their proposals you will be asked to give the times at which the bombardments should take place.
An isolation barrage of the objective by the Divisional Artillery will begin at once and continue uninterruptedly.

(iv). You will make arrangements for medium trench mortar cooperation at once.

2. It must be impressed on all ranks that the above is important and calls for just as much self sacrifice and devotion as an attack. Work must be carried on in spite of the enemy. At the same time the latter should be harassed by constant artillery and machine gun fire especially at night. Points from which his line can be enfiladed or overlooked should be sought for.

26th Aug., 1916.

Lieut. Colonel,
General Staff, 15th Division.

Copy to :-

C.R.E.
C.R.A. Left Group R.A.

**HEADQUARTERS,
15th DIVISION.
26 AUG 1916**

**III CORPS
GENERAL STAFF.
"O."
G.698.
No. ....
Date. 26.8.16.**

15th. Division.
****

1. When you have taken over the line at present held by the 1st. Division, the Corps Commander wishes you to work on the following plan :

    (a) Continue to prolong Clark's Trench (approximates S.2.d.9.9.) so as to join it up with the Switch Line about S.2.a.9.2.

    (b) Push forward from this line towards the high ground about S.3.a.5.9. in order to obtain a position for gaining the Switch Line in M.33.C. and D. There is already a post in S.3.b. which should be extended to both flanks as an advanced line to Clark's Trench. The 1st. Division on your right will be ordered to gain the northern edge of HIGH WOOD and to connect up with your right on the SWITCH LINE.

    (c) Push out strong Posts from CAMERON TRENCH so as to form a line 200 yards from the new German trench S.W. of MARTINPUICH.

    (d) If the situation in the INTERMEDIATE LINE has not been cleared up by the time you take over, to gain possession of this trench and join it up by communication trenches to CLARK'S TRENCH.

2. It must be impressed on Commanders and their troops that the above work is important and calls for just as much self sacrifice and devotion as an attack. Work must be carried on in spite of the enemy. At the same time the latter should be harassed by constant artillery and machine gun fire especially at night. Points from which his line can be enfiladed or overlooked should be sought for.

H.Q. III Corps.

26th. August, 1916.

Brigadier-General,
General Staff,
III Corps.

Copies for information to :-

    1st. Division.
    B.G.R.A.
    C.E.

My dear Knox

Of course I have foreseen this for some days & think
of little else —

(1) To begin to grumble privately — 1st Div. have no trenches
no communications — no places from which to start. Therefore
danger of any attack being destroyed prior to its advance
owing the difficulty of hiding any assembly beforehand —
The slight rise is an advantage which I didn't realize —
But even so to make a good job of it trenches should
first be cut as shown .... Dumps at X —
Food — bombs S.A.A. — water. This means 1500 yards
approx. of trenches and 4 Dumps —
All this irrespective of work on the rest of the line
e.g. 6th Avenue in S2d. Lancs. Trench. Lancs Sap
Pioneer alley all require an enormous amount of
work — & men are taken from my Bn. daily for
extraneous purposes. Corps cable. Div. O.P. Dugouts
etc — And I must not men or we shall get as
tired as others —

Therefore I am of opinion that 29th is too early

unless others are to be at hand to consolidate.

2/ I think dark to consolidate in.

3/ Don't you rather think that the line Anderson SAP to 1st Div. SAP. a little too ambitious for the first jump men would lose their way. I would rather follow the contour of the hill which run as as I have shown — . — . — at any rate at first — & in first instance would only cut across the angle, otherwise we might be digging in too close to HILL TOP. ridge which looks formidable —

4/ Let our Artillery from now on keep hammering away & making the whole intermediate line unlivable in — just like she did prior to SWITCH. & Just advertise the assault.

5/ The difficulty of assembly prior to assault is far more difficult than the assault in these bad trenches —

6/. DO come & see me tea time this afternoon.

Yrs ever.

Musanyood

BOTTOM TRENCH EAST

HILL TOP TR:

ANDERSON TRENCH   ANDERSON SAP

1st DIV SAP

INTERMEDIATE LINE

ROMEO ALLEY

LANCS SAP

Slight rise which breaks
INTERMEDIATE LINE obs: visible
from our front

(a)

SECRET.

Headquarters,
15th. Division.
26th. August 16.

My dear General,

1. The signs of the times seem to point to the probability of the honour of capturing the INTERMEDIATE LINE falling to the 15th. Division. The 1st. Division may or may not take it. It is as well however that we should start to consider how the job is to be done.

2. The G.O.C. is quite decided that if we attack it is to be a proper assault and not an idiotic raid. He also thinks we should make one job of it and clear the whole area together.

3. The Corps have mentioned that if we undertake it, the probable date will be the 29th. There are other operations that day. The time I do not know. Let us, however, in our preliminary consideration of the problem, ignore other operations and decide how we would best like to carry it out if left entirely independent. This is of course only a preliminary discussion.

4. The following proposals are for your consideration :-

Reference :-
Rough sketch attached.

(i). During next few days Heavy Artillery to systematically bombard the INTERMEDIATE LINE, POINT (a), and HILL TOP TRENCH.
You to say which hours most convenient to you to evacuate trenches within 200 yards.

(ii). Medium trench mortars to assist where objective can be reached by them.

(iii). Divisional Artillery to keep constant fire on the approaches to the INTERMEDIATE LINE to prevent reinforcements and supplies reaching the garrison.

(iv). Work on trench east of PIONEER ALLEY to be pushed on and it is to be connected with LANCS SAP as a jumping off place.

(v). The assault to be carried out at zero hour by about two battalions - one from ~~east~~ (west) and one from the south. An intense double barrage to open at zero and the assaulting troops to go in with it.

(vi). At zero hour every gun we can raise to fire on HIGH WOOD, HILL TOP TRENCH and on south of MARTINPUICH.

(vii). Is a smoke barrage advisable ?. If so, where ?.

(viii). The supporting wave of the right battalion to push right forward and dig in on the line 1st. Division Sap ANDERSON SAP which should be pushed on all we can in the meantime.
Advanced posts and barrage to be kept in front of them.

(ix). What time should zero be ?. 8.30 a.m.? mid-day ?.

5. I write pusposely rather than come to see you so that when we meet we can thrash it out properly.

Where can I come to see you ?.

Yours Sincerely,

BGRA

Lieut-Genl D.H.

A copy of a letter sent today
to 45th Inf Bde for your information
Please return

26/8/16

See EWS
26.8.16

www.ingramcontent.com/pod-product-compliance
Lightning Source LLC
Chambersburg PA
CBHW081359160426
43193CB00013B/2068